TWAYNE'S WORLD LEADERS SERIES

EDITORS OF THIS VOLUME

Arthur W. Brown

Baruch College, The City University

of New York

and

Thomas S. Knight

Adelphi University

Charles de Gaulle

Charles de Gaulle

Charles de Gaulle

RONALD C. MONTICONE

Queensborough Community College
The City University of New York

TWAYNE PUBLISHERS

A DIVISION OF G. K. HALL & CO., BOSTON

Library of Congress Cataloging in Publication Data

Monticone, Ronald C.
  Charles de Gaulle.

  (Twayne's world leaders series)
  Includes bibliographical references.
  1. Gaulle, Charles de, Pres. France, 1890-1970. 2. France
—Foreign relations—1945-   2-5-76
DC373.G3M63   944.083'092'4   (B)   74-16412
ISBN 0-8057-3663-8

Contents

About the Author

Ronald C. Monticone is presently an Associate Professor of Government at the Queensborough Division of the City University of New York. He received his B.A. and M.A. degrees in Political Science from the University of Maryland, where he was a graduate fellow, and a Ph.D. from the Department of Government and International Relations of New York University.

The author received two research fellowships from the State of New York for the summers of 1968 and 1969. Since 1966, he has been Editorial Assistant of the *Polish Review*, a scholarly quarterly on Polish and East European Affairs. Several of his articles on Poland and Eastern Europe were published in the *Review*.

Professor Monticone has travelled extensively in Eastern and Western Europe and in Latin America. Research on this work was conducted at the Library of Congress in Washington, D.C., the New York Public Library, the French Embassy, the Bibliothèque Nationale in Paris and the Lenin Library in Moscow.

Preface

Recent historians have often contended that Charles de Gaulle was a mystery wrapped in an enigma who few people if any knew or understood. He has been portrayed as a proud, austere introvert, a cold and calculating politician easily taking offense, vengeful but moreover a nationalist if not a chauvinist. Although there is some truth in these contentions, it is my sincere belief that each one is either an exaggeration or an oversimplification of the fact. Neither was de Gaulle's foreign policy, which took first place in his order of priorities, as complex as many historians assert. In this book, I attempt to analyze in an objective manner the policies of this most misunderstood and often maligned statesman.

De Gaulle's foreign policy becomes less complex when one considers that his one aim was greater prestige and influence for France, although his means of achieving this goal varied from year to year. It should be recalled that French hegemony over Western and Central Europe, which had been established as a result of the Thirty Years' War (1618-1648), lasted two and one-quarter centuries and collapsed when Emperor Napoleon III and his entire army were forced to surrender to the Prussians at Sedan on September 2, 1870. The German states (excluding Austria), which had been struggling for unity under Prussian leadership for more than two decades, were soon united into a single nation and replaced France as the most powerful entity economically and militarily on the European continent. Germany remained predominant in Europe, except for a short interval after her defeat in World War I, until her final defeat in World War II.

De Gaulle realized that Germany's defeat in the Second World War and her subsequent division created for France an opportunity to regain her former position as the leading force in Western

Europe. But this opportunity was conditional on first freeing the nations of Western Europe from their status as satellites of the United States, and then rallying them around France. Although de Gaulle believed that each nation should remain entirely sovereign, he felt that eventually Western Europe would follow the political leadership of France.

While attempting to end American hegemony and rally Western Europe around France, he sought a détente with the Communist nations of Eastern Europe. France and Eastern Europe (including Russia) had been traditional allies mainly because they felt threatened by the economic and military power of Germany, regardless of whether that Germany was governed by Wilhelm II or Hitler. But, with the coming of the Cold War in 1948, most of the ties between France and Eastern Europe were ended. After the period of the "Thaw" in Eastern Europe, which put an end to Stalinism, de Gaulle felt that it was time to restore the traditional ties between France and these nations.

A good portion of this book is devoted to de Gaulle's attempt to rebuild the traditional political, economic, cultural, scientific, and technological ties between France and Eastern Europe. This policy is known as détente. He believed that other Western nations would then follow France's lead. Détente would simply serve as a prelude to an entente between the nations of Eastern and Western Europe, followed by cooperation among all nations of Europe regardless of their socioeconomic and political systems. De Gaulle envisaged sometime in the future not a Europe divided into two parts, one dominated by the United States and the other by the Soviet Union, but instead one Europe from the Atlantic to the Urals, in which each nation would cooperate with every other in all realms.

Although many people feel that Europe from the Atlantic to the Urals is a utopian ideal, it is their misunderstanding of de Gaulle's plan ("Grand Design") that leads them to this conclusion. The feasibility of his "Grand Design" is analyzed in the course of this work.

Acknowledgments

I wish to acknowledge my gratitude to the entire staff of the Service de Presse et d'Information of the French Embassy in New York for the numerous documents they supplied to me over a period of many months and without which this work could not have been completed.

I am also deeply indebted to my wife for correcting the numerous texts I was required to translate from French into English.

Chronology

1890 Born November 22 in Lille, France, son of Henri de Gaulle and Jeanne Maillot.

1910 Enters French military academy of Saint-Cyr.

1913 Joins 33rd Infantry regiment as sub-lieutenant, commanded by Pétain.

1916 Captured at Verdun and imprisoned at Ingolstadt, Bavaria.

1918 Returns to the home of his family in Dordogne after the signing of the armistice.

1919-

1920 Attached to Weygand's mission in Poland and becomes instructor at Polish War School.

1921 Marries Yvonne Vendroux.
Becomes professor of military history at Saint-Cyr.

1922 Enters Ecole Supérieure de la guerre.

1925 Joins Pétain's staff at Superior War Council.

1927 Promoted to the rank of major and permitted to give a series of lectures at the Senior War School.

1932 Appointed Secretary of Superior Council of National Defense and promoted to the rank of lieutenant colonel; publishes *Le Fil de l'Epée*.

1934 Publishes *Vers l'Armée de Métier*.

1937 Becomes commander of 507th tank regiment at Metz and is promoted to the rank of colonel.

1938 Publishes *La France et son Armée*.

1940 May—Commands 4th Armored Division in battles of Moncornet and Laon. June—Becomes under-secretary of war in Reynaud cabinet. June 18—Flees to London and appeals for continued resistance in a broadcast.

1942 Free French not included in invasion of North Africa.

1943 Summoned to Casablanca Conference in January.
Formation of French Committee of National Liberation at Algiers in June.

1944 Returns to liberated Paris in August.

Visits Moscow for talks with Stalin in December.

1945 Not invited to Yalta or Potsdam conferences.

1946 Resigns as leader of France.

1947 Founds Rally of the French People (RPF).

1954 Publishes *Mémoires de Guerre*.

1955 Retires to Colombey-les-deux-Eglises.

1958 Algerian uprising.

Becomes last prime minister of the Fourth Republic in June.

1959 Elected president of the Fifth Republic in January.

Offers Algeria the right to self-determination in September.

1960 Visits the United States and Great Britain.

1961 Puts down generals' revolt in Algeria.

1962 Evian Agreements signed in March.

Algeria becomes independent in July.

1963 Vetoes British entry into Common Market; signs Treaty of Cooperation with Federal Republic of Germany.

1965 Announces in September that France will no longer participate in NATO when the treaty expires in 1969 but will begin withdrawal of troops from integrated NATO command immediately.

Elected President of France in December.

1966 Visit to Russia.

1967 Visit to Poland.

1968 Visit to Rumania in May.

Dissolves parliament in June and calls for new elections because of spring riots.

Gaullists receive greatest majority ever in the June elections.

1969 Resigns as president of France in April and retires to Colombey-les-deux-Eglises.

1970 Dies November 10 in Colombey-les-deux-Eglises.

CHAPTER 1

De Gaulle the Man

F RANÇOIS Guizot, chief minister of King Louis Philippe of France between 1840 and 1848, is said to have made the following statement to Lord Aberdeen on September 16, 1849, after Louis Philippe, had abdicated and Guizot was no longer in power: "You may count on the fact that foreign policy does not concern the French at all and will not be the cause of any important event. Governments can do what they please. If they make foolish mistakes they will not be supported; if they are stupid they will be hissed at without anger and without being overthrown as a result. The only ones (governments) that are taken seriously are those that accomplish something in terms of domestic affairs of the country."[1]

No person could possibly disagree more with this statement than Charles de Gaulle, who saw foreign policy as the center, the focus of all political thought. For him, the government is conceived in terms of foreign policy. This idea can be seen in his almost total emphasis on foreign policy not only throughout his eleven years as president of the Fifth Republic of France and his two years as leader of France between 1944 and 1946 but during a much earlier period in his life. The fact that he was foreign-policy oriented should come as no surprise to anyone who is acquainted with his early life, since he was a military scientist and military historian and the author of several books on military science and history at a time when he was still relatively unknown.

Characteristics

It has often been said that Charles de Gaulle was a man of yesterday. But he was a man of tomorrow as well. He was a man who liked to impersonate the heir of the old kings of France but who, at the same time, wished to be the ruler of a thoroughly modern and efficient state.[2]

He was definitely a man who moved with the times: a man with a great deal of flexibility in spite of his outward appearance. He was a profound thinker throughout his entire life, and in his seventh decade he learned more about the erosion of power blocs that emerged as a result of World War II than many Cold War rulers of other Western nations who were chronologically twenty years his junior. He believed as early as 1944 in decolonization, and as president of France succeeded in making his country the best liked of the Western nations in the Third World as well as in the Communist bloc countries.

There was no doubt in the mind of Charles de Gaulle that France must be the leading nation of Western Europe and should achieve this position if necessary through close agreement with West Germany. But de Gaulle felt that France must not be either an American or a Russian satellite. He was not anti-American or anti-British. He simply did not consider these to be European nations, whereas Russia was fundamentally European.

To de Gaulle, ideologies were the most unstable elements in the world; the most stable were nations. To de Gaulle, Ho Chi Minh was more of an anti-Chinese Vietnamese nationalist than a Communist. The United States was driving him into the arms of the Chinese.[3] De Gaulle felt that in spite of her new ideology, Russia would one day turn to Europe, not to Asia, since she is culturally part of Europe.

De Gaulle has been called anti-American but this contention is not completely true. At the time of the Cuban missile crisis of 1962, he made it quite clear that France was on the side of the United States.

De Gaulle was not a hater. Apart from the monstrosities of history, de Gaulle hated only one man: Franklin D. Roosevelt, who persisted in humiliating de Gaulle scores upon scores of times. To any objective individual who knows the facts of this story, one can hardly blame de Gaulle.

He did not divide humanity into good and bad categories. The interests of France came first. He would make an alliance with any nation if he felt it was in the interest of his country. De Gaulle liked all races and nationalities. Felix Eboué, the black governor of Chad, went over to the Free French in July, 1940, and became a close friend of de Gaulle. He always considered blacks equal to whites. In his later years, de Gaulle was accused of being anti-Semitic because of his policies toward Israel. The truth of the matter is that he never showed any anti-Semitism, and did his utmost to stamp it out among the Free French in London. His later policies toward Israel were based on factors other than anti-Semitism.

De Gaulle was a very religious man throughout his life. There was a rich store of Christian charity in him that did not openly manifest itself. We cannot attribute his attitude toward the peoples of the Third World solely to hard-headed political calculation. He was conscious of the plight of the human beings who inhabited the Third World and felt very deeply for their well-being.

There was within de Gaulle a strain of liberalism that often got him into trouble with the army. Even though he was a professional army man, the biggest quarrels of his life were with the army.[4] Although, paradoxically, when he returned to become president of the Fifth Republic of France, he preferred to be called "general" rather than "president," he had built up a strong resentment toward the army leaders for the disgrace they had brought upon France. They were wrong about Dreyfus; they were wrong about the Maginot Line; they were wrong about a strictly defensive policy and the appeasement of Hitler in the 1930's; and they were wrong about Vichy. By the time of the Algerian crisis, de Gaulle believed that the credibility of the army leaders was nil. He knew the Algerians were fighting primarily for their national identity, while the army leaders felt that France was fighting world communism in Algeria. History has again proved de Gaulle correct about Algeria, and the army leaders wrong.

It is now time to give a brief biographical sketch of Charles de Gaulle, from his earliest years through World War II, before going on to discuss his policy toward the USSR, Europe, and the United States.

Early Life

Charles de Gaulle was born at Lille on November 22, 1890. His father, Henri de Gaulle, served as a colonel in the French army and then became a teacher of philosophy, mathematics, and literature at a Jesuit college in Paris. Since Henri de Gaulle

and his wife Jeanne Maillot were devout Catholics, Henri offered
his services to the Jesuit collège although he would have preferred a career in the army.

Charles de Gaulle grew up in an atmosphere that was as religious as it was military. The de Gaulles were one of the oldest and
most prominent families of Normandy and had been identified
with the story of France for many centuries. Seigneur de Gaulle
was a lieutenant for Charles VI of France and defended Porte
Saint-Denis against the attacking forces of Burgundy in 1414.
Jean de Gaulle was one of the French noblemen who had engaged in the Battle of Agincourt. During the Hundred Years'
War, Jean de Gaulle refused to take an oath of allegiance to King
Henry V of England after his victory in Normandy, and as a result, the English king confiscated his lands and goods. Many
years later when the war ended in a French victory, Jean de
Gaulle was rewarded by the king of France with a fief of land in
Burgundy.[5]

Charles de Gaulle enjoyed telling all of these stories. He was
reading the history of France at the age of five. One day, he
came across a book written by his grandfather entitled *Nouvelle
Histoire de Paris*. He became interested in the city and its envi-
rons and regarded the Invalides, Versailles, the Luxembourg, the
Arch of Triumph, the Cathedral of Notre Dame, and the Abbey
of Saint-Denis as symbols of the past glories of France. But in
these symbols, he was able to see the errors and failings of his
country. He was upset about the defeat of France in the
Franco-Prussian War of 1870 and the humiliation France suffered
at Fashoda in 1898 when she backed down to avoid a war with
Great Britain.

At the age of ten, Charles played soldiers as readily as other
boys, but he played it not as a game but as a lesson in the art of
military science. He became the leader in his neighborhood, and
it was astonishing how boys four and five years his senior obeyed
his orders. He had an instinctive and powerful gift of leadership.[6]

Henri de Gaulle was firm but affectionate with his children. As
the years passed, he found himself drawing closer and closer to
Charles. Henri and Charles discussed the Dreyfus case, which
was reopened when Charles was fifteen. Dreyfus was found innocent after having served a long sentence in exile on Devil's Island. The fact that this innocent Jewish officer could have been
originally sentenced on the basis of evidence forged against him

by certain army officials horrified Charles, who was imbued with the principles of honor and justice.

By this time, Charles had decided to become a professional soldier. He received his secondary education at Jesuit collèges, first at his father's school and then, when it was closed in 1907, at a Jesuit collège in Belgium. Upon graduation, he returned to Paris to prepare for the entrance examination at the notable military school of St. Cyr. He passed the entrance examination in August, 1909, but because of a recent law, had to spend a year in the army as an ordinary soldier. Charles chose the 33rd Regiment of Infantry at Arras. He did not give any indication during his year at Arras of being a good soldier, let alone a great one. He was described by his commanding officer as untidy and unruly. Actually, Charles was already rebelling against what he considered the nonessentials of army life. He believed that a soldier's first duty was to be trained in the art of war, which was continuously changing with the times. After the completion of one year at Arras, he spent two years at St. Cyr and graduated among the top ten in his class. Upon graduation he returned to his old regiment as a sub-lieutenant.

Charles de Gaulle was twenty-three years of age when World War I broke out. It just so happened that the commander of his regiment at the time was Colonel Pétain. The latter was told that in his command there was a young officer whose most striking characteristic was his originality of thought. Pétain came to know and like de Gaulle for his strict discipline mixed with sympathy and understanding for the ordinary soldier. They spoke about various subjects but particularly of France, her history, and the French army.

De Gaulle came to the conclusion that Pétain was France's greatest general in World War I. He considered Pétain one of the few generals who understood long before 1914 the coming clash with Germany and the inadequacy of French military equipment. It was Pétain who had foreseen the need for heavy artillery.

On March 2, 1916, de Gaulle was wounded at Verdun and taken prisoner by the Germans. He made several attempts to escape but each time his height was a barrier. Finally, he was imprisoned in Ingolstadt, Bavaria, where officers who had made several attempts to escape were confined. At Ingolstadt he became acquainted with General Catroux, who, twenty-four years later, would be the only five-star general to join the Free French, and a Russian officer who later became Soviet Marshal Tukhachevsky.

Captain de Gaulle was a very sick man when he returned to the home of his family in the Dordogne after the signing of the armistice. He was suffering from the effects of poor food and long months of captivity. But by the winter of 1919 he was ready for duty again. Polish General Joseph Haller was organizing the Fifth Division of Chasseurs at Sille-le-Guillaume and was enroute to Poland, which was then at war with Russia for the return of certain lands in the east that the Bolshevik government refused to relinquish. After being moved to Poland, this division fought the Russians, first in Volhynia and then in the Battle of the Vistula, where Weygand became the French military adviser to Pilsudski.[7] De Gaulle, who had joined this division, was impressed by the poverty-stricken Polish peasants who fought for Poland and remained immune to Bolshevik propaganda. In de Gaulle's mind, this was simply another manifestation of nationalism, the most unifying of all forces.

De Gaulle Begins His Career

On his return to France in November, 1920, de Gaulle became acquainted with Yvonne Vendroux, daughter of a Calais industrialist. They were married in 1921. After his marriage, he taught military history at St. Cyr for a short time and then spent two years as a student at the Ecole Supérieure de la guerre, the staff college for the officer elite.[8] His teachers agreed that he was brilliant, intelligent, and highly cultured, but because of his nonconformism, he was awarded grades lower than those he had earned. This unfairness angered Philippe Pétain, who had by this time become not only a notable general but a personal friend of de Gaulle and godfather of his oldest son, Philippe, born in 1921. Pétain tried in vain to get the teaching staff to change his grades.

In 1925, Pétain became vice-president of the War Council and appointed Captain de Gaulle to his secretariat. De Gaulle then began to write lectures on French military history. In 1927, he was promoted to the rank of major, and Pétain demanded that de Gaulle be allowed to give a series of lectures on leadership at the Ecole Supérieure. Pétain was obviously attempting to vindicate the scandal of de Gaulle's grades at the Ecole Supérieure, which prevented him from becoming a teacher at the Staff College.

The demand was not received well, but de Gaulle was allowed to give the lectures, which were later incorporated into his famous book *Le Fil de l'Epée*, published in 1932.

According to one biographer of de Gaulle:

The Edge of the Sword attracted a great deal of attention. It has since always been regarded as de Gaulle's most striking declaration of his faith and beliefs. In its pages the character of the man is revealed time and time again and in all its many sides. His scholarship is shown in the turn of phrase, the selection of adjectives, the breadth of example. His study of philosophy is also revealed here. The man of religion and of brotherhood shines out from the pages of his book. There also are the lonely man and the man who would treasure friends. Above all, de Gaulle demonstrated in *The Edge of the Sword* that he was a wise man. But, unten and understand.[9]

In 1932, Charles de Gaulle was appointed secretary-general of the Council for National Defense at the request of Generals Pétain and Weygand and promoted to the rank of lieutenant colonel. This position brought de Gaulle into close contact with the political leaders and with military planning. He began to realize that France was growing weaker while Germany was growing stronger each year. Even though France did have the greatest army in Europe, it was not inevitable that this military superiority would last forever.

In 1934, de Gaulle's second famous book, *Vers l'Armée de Métier* (The Army of the Future), was published. This book was a complete appraisal of the military situation as it affected France. De Gaulle spoke of the ineffectiveness of the Maginot Line, which extended between the Moselle and the Rhine and then along the Rhine itself, because the line was never extended along the Franco-Belgian border. This fault should have been seen by anyone with a minimum of common sense, but this was not the view held by the army leaders. Not only could the Maginot Line be bypassed through Belgium, which Germany had invaded during World War I, but the current French military system based on the defense of France's frontiers did not take into account France's allies in Eastern Europe. De Gaulle warned in his book that France was part of an established order in Europe and could not confine herself to the defense of her frontiers. He warned that the French had shed blood and tears in 1870-1871 for having given Prussia a free hand against Austria in 1866. This seemed to be a clear warning against letting Hitler reoccupy the Rhineland in 1936, Austria in 1938, and Czechoslovakia in 1938-1939.

De Gaulle also argued that the French army was composed of men who did not have enough experience in handling weapons of modern warfare, and advocated the creation of a powerful striking force that should be ready to invade Germany if necessary. He did not fail to call this striking force preventive, either. At the same time he called for the creation of a professional army.

De Gaulle's book made little impact on France, since she was suffering from an anti-war psychosis. She had lost more than one and one-half million men in World War I and could not bring herself to think of having to fight another war within a generation. His proposals were opposed not only from the Left but also by the French generals. The Left feared that a professional army might well become the guardian of a fascist regime.

Within the government, only Paul Reynaud, the minister of justice, took de Gaulle's proposals seriously, but parliament was unwilling to listen. French military strategy was based on the defensive policy of the Maginot Line, and billions were spent on this defense. The belief was that since France was not vulnerable to invasion, why spend additional billions on an offensive policy. Hitler was able to draw his own conclusions, and on March 7 1936, reoccupied the Rhineland.

French public opinion seemed to be totally indifferent to all international events. In the May, 1936, elections the Popular Front of the socialist leader Léon Blum won. De Gaulle failed to convince him of the need for the creation of a professional army and a powerful striking force. Blum argued that France could do little to protect Eastern Europe from a German invasion but that Germany would fail in the long run since the Maginot Line made France invincible. De Gaulle could not have disagreed more.

When the Popular Front of Léon Blum ended in 1937 and new elections brought to power the Radical Socialists led by Daladier, de Gaulle was promoted to the rank of colonel and placed in command of a tank regiment at Metz. The purpose of his promotion and reassignment was to get him out of Paris, the mainstream of French political life, since Daladier regarded him as an agitator and wished to relocate him far from the places where decisions were made. Soon enough came Anschluss, Munich, and the invasion of Poland, and France again found herself at war.

De Gaulle did not blame Stalin for signing a nonaggression pact with Hitler in 1939. He mentions in his *Mémoires* that Stalin had come to the conclusion that France would not lift a finger to defend Eastern Europe; therefore he had one of two choices: either make an agreement with Hitler to share in the spoils or become Hitler's victim along with the others. It was only logical that Stalin should choose the former.[10]

Free France

With the fall of France in June, 1940, to the German invaders, the French people became bitter, hostile, and angry: angry with the press, angry with the politicians, and especially angry with the generals. All three had defended the Maginot Line theory, which had proved to be a myth. The Germans again invaded France via the Belgian frontier, which had been the missing link in the Maginot Line. De Gaulle had been correct all along in warning that the Maginot Line could be bypassed through Belgium. He had been correct throughout the 1930's in contending that France was part of an established order in Europe and could not confine herself to the defense of her frontiers. He had cried out against the appeasement of Hitler in 1938. The generals had been wrong on both counts.

Several days before the capitulation, General Weygand told Colonel de Gaulle that England would sue for peace with Germany within a week and the war would come to an end. Vichy was the best the generals could hope to do for France under these most unfortunate circumstances. Under the terms of the armistice that followed, Northern France was occupied by German troops, while the southern half, which was unoccupied, was transformed into an authoritarian regime with its capital at Vichy, headed by the then senile Marshal Pétain and the cynical and unscrupulous politician Pierre Laval. De Gaulle never regarded the Vichy regime as anything but a puppet of Nazi Germany.

Before de Gaulle took his courageous stand and fled to England on June 18, surrounding himself with French soldiers, officers, engineers, and armaments workers who had been evacuated from the beaches of Dunkirk several days earlier, he had seen Churchill three times and was convinced that England would continue the war.

Only two hours after Marshal Pétain's broadcast appeal on June 18 from Bordeaux—"It is with a broken heart that I tell you today that combat must cease"—Charles de Gaulle addressed the French nation from London as follows:

The leaders who, for many years past, have been at the head of the French armed forces, have set up a government.

Alleging the defeat of our armies, this government has entered into negotiations with the enemy with a view to bringing about a cessation of hostilities. It is quite true that we were, and still are, overwhelmed by enemy mechanized forces, both on the ground and in the air. It was the tanks, the planes, and the tactics of the Germans, far more than the fact that we were outnumbered, that forced our armies to retreat. It was the German tanks, planes and tactics that provided the element of surprise which brought our leaders to their present plight.

But has the last word been said? Must we abandon all hope? Is our defeat final and irremediable? To those questions I answer—NO!

Speaking in full knowledge of the facts, I ask you to believe me when I say that the cause of France is not lost. The very factors that brought about our defeat may one day lead us to victory.

For, remember this, France does not stand alone. Behind her is a vast Empire, and she can make common cause with the British Empire, which commands the seas and is continuing the struggle. Like England, she can draw unreservedly on the immense industrial resources of the United States.

This war is not limited to our unfortunate country. The outcome of the struggle has not been decided by the Battle of France. This is a world war. Mistakes have been made, there have been delays and untold suffering, but the fact remains that there still exists in the world everything we need to crush our enemies some day. Today we are crushed by the sheer weight of mechanized force hurled against us, but we can still look to a future in which even greater mechanized force will bring us victory. The destiny of the world is at stake.

I, General de Gaulle, now in London, call on all French officers and men who are at present on British soil, or may be in the future, with or without their arms; I call on all engineers and skilled workmen from the armaments factories who are at present on British soil, or may be in the future, to get in touch with me.

Whatever happens, the flame of French resistance must not and shall not die.[11]

There was a degree of uneasiness on the part of the English government in receiving de Gaulle on June 18, 1940, and in putting the facilities of the BBC at his disposal. London did not wish to antagonize the newly established Vichy government of France, which Hitler was trying to turn against Great Britain. On June

28, the English government took the daring step and recognized Charles de Gaulle as leader of the Free French.

Hitler preferred the Vichy solution rather than the occupation of all of France. It was more economical for Germany. Harsher terms might have resulted in the entire French fleet's going over to London.[12]

De Gaulle truly understood political realities, unlike the other generals. On June 30, 1940, when he recruited a number of civilians into his camp, he remarked to Maurice Schumann, member of the Paris Christian Democratic group: "If Hitler had meant to come to London, he would already be here. I think that Russia will come into the war before America, but they will both come in. Hitler is thinking of the Ukraine. He won't be able to resist the temptation to settle things with Russia and that will be the beginning of his downfall. . . . In short, the war is a terrible problem but it is already decided. What remains to be done is to bring all of France over to the right side."[13]

De Gaulle was in a very difficult position in 1940 as leader of the Free French. The Dutch, Belgians, Norwegians, Poles, and Czechoslovaks all had governments-in-exile. Their nations were temporarily under German occupation. The Belgian government still controlled the Congo, while the Dutch controlled Indonesia. On the other hand, there was still a government in France that was recognized by many nations in the world including the United States and the USSR. The French Empire would by the end of 1940 be split almost down the middle. In general, the Arabs in North Africa remained loyal to Vichy while most of Black Africa, which for legitimate reasons was anti-Nazi, preferred the Free French. Felix Eboué, governor of Chad, came over to de Gaulle very early; on July 16, 1940, and again on August 26, Eboué proclaimed the adherence of his colony to Free France.

That same night (August 26) Leclerc and Boislambert, two of de Gaulle's officers, made contact with the authorities in Douala on the coast of the Cameroons and the following day headed for Yaoundé, the capital. The authorities officially recognized the Free French. Two days later on August 28, Larminat, another Free French official, went to Brazzaville, capital of French Equitorial Africa, and the authorities there received the Free French with even greater enthusiasm than those in Chad and the Cameroons. On August 29, the governor of Gambon renounced his allegiance to Vichy and declared in favor of the Free French.

However, complications began at this point. The naval commander at Libreville, capital of Gambon, remained loyal to Vichy and
forced the governor to reverse his decision.

De Gaulle proposed that the English and the Free French attempt to seize Dakar, the point in Africa nearest the American
continent. Strategically, Dakar was very important, and the
British government could not resist the venture. Churchill
realized that Dakar was heavily fortified, and he was taking a
gamble that Vichy would not retaliate against a British attack by
declaring war.[14] A battleship appeared off the coast of Dakar on
September 23, and several emissaries of the Free French disem-
barked carrying a white flag. Nevertheless, they were fired upon
and wounded. Heavy fighting followed and several British and
Vichy submarines were sunk. The expedition ended in failure and
Dakar remained Vichy.

But the enterprise was not in vain. The Free French, who had
failed to take Dakar, consolidated their efforts in Central Africa,
and in a bloody battle with Vichy troops succeeded in taking back
Gambon.

September proved to be a good month for the Free French
when the French Islands in the Pacific, including the New Heb-
rides, Tahiti, and New Caledonia, declared their allegiance to the
Free French.

It was in Brazzaville, capital of French Equatorial Africa, that
de Gaulle created his Council for the Defense of the Empire on
October 22, 1940. Brazzaville became the birthplace of Free
France and the cradle of decolonization.

When Russia entered the war in June, 1941, de Gaulle was
very much aware that the real war was now being fought in Russia, not in Africa. De Gaulle requested that the Free French be
allowed to send three representatives to Moscow who would
serve as direct liaison between the Soviet Union and the Free
French. In this request, de Gaulle stressed that France and the
USSR were continental powers with problems very different from
those of the British. Even in 1941, de Gaulle felt that victory
over the Germans would create a number of problems for France
and the USSR, the two continental powers, which the United
States and Great Britain could not understand. Moscow agreed to
receive the three representatives of the Free French.

When de Gaulle and the Free French formed the French National Committee, a sort of provisional cabinet in exile, in Sep-

tember, 1941, it was recognized not only by the Russians but also by the British, who had never recognized Vichy. However, the United States continued to maintain diplomatic relations with the Vichy regime and refused to recognize the French National Committee. This policy was a constant reminder to de Gaulle of Roosevelt's dislike for him, a dislike which would have far-reaching ramifications on Franco-American relations throughout his eleven years as president of the Fifth Republic of France many years later.

De Gaulle was ready to associate the Free French directly with the war in Russia. He felt that the British did not understand land warfare since Great Britain was an island, and that therefore only the USSR could defeat Germany. Actually, de Gaulle wanted to send one of the two French divisions in Syria to the USSR. Both French divisions were, however, under British command, and since the British raised objections to sending the French division to the USSR, Moscow had to reject the offer but did so under pressure.

Throughout the war de Gaulle complained to Moscow about the attitude of the British and the Americans and how they were attempting to reduce the Free French to a strictly military organization devoid of any political objectives. He joined hands with the Russians in continuing to pressure the British and the Americans into establishing the second front. At one point (June, 1942) de Gaulle became convinced that the British were about to invade Niger and the Americans, Dakar without participation by the Free French. De Gaulle then approached Mr. Bogomolov, Soviet ambassador to the various governments-in-exile in London, and told him that if the above were to come to pass, he would break with the British and the Americans. He also requested that in such an event the Soviet government admit him and the army of the Free French on Soviet territory. However, before the Soviet government even had time to reply, the entire incident blew over once the American and British governments assured de Gaulle that no maneuvers would take place in North Africa without a consultation with the Free French.

De Gaulle also made clear to Mr. Bogomolov that he was anxious to rally around him all Frenchmen willing to fight the Germans, including French Communists. The Resistance leaders in France were in close contact with the Free French.

In July, 1942, de Gaulle decided to rename the Free French

Movement "Fighting France." Immediately the USSR endorsed this change in name and recognized Fighting France as including all French citizens and territories. This action meant that Moscow recognized de Gaulle's authority over the entire Resistance movement, which included French Communists. The American and British recognition of Fighting France was not quite so pronounced, and de Gaulle had reason to believe that the Americans and British were searching for a third solution for France, one other than Vichy or the Free French.

De Gaulle had reason to be suspicious. In November, 1942, Anglo-American forces landed in Morocco and Algeria and forced the Vichy authorities to abandon their neutral stand toward the Germans. Within three days of the Allied landing in North Africa, Hitler occupied Vichy France. At this point, it became more difficult to maintain the fiction of an independent Vichy France even though the Vichy government remained. The United States had no other choice than to recall its ambassador to Vichy. Nevertheless, Roosevelt's attitude toward de Gaulle remained implacable and the former refused to recognize the French National Committee. The part of the French Empire that had remained loyal to the Vichy regime now openly broke with Vichy and jumped on the bandwagon of the Allies.

The chief problem of the Anglo-Americans was to find a French leader who could rally the French authorities in North Africa. De Gaulle and the Free French could be of no use, since this had been Vichy territory, and a former move by de Gaulle to establish himself at Dakar clearly demonstrated that the French colonial administrators remained mostly loyal to Vichy. Therefore the Anglo-Americans enlisted General Henri Giraud, a five-star general who had escaped from internment in Germany in the spring of 1942 but had not joined the Free French. Instead, he had fled to Vichy and declared his allegiance to Pétain. Giraud landed secretly in Algeria on November 5, 1942. To complicate matters, Admiral Darlan, formerly commander in chief of all Vichy forces, appeared on the scene, but he was cooperative and helped to rally French North Africa to the Allies. He had for a while been premier of Vichy under Pétain and his record was somewhat embarrassing to the Allies. Darlan became supreme ruler in North Africa and reluctantly agreed, on General Eisenhower's urging, to have Giraud appointed French commander in chief in North Africa. When Darlan was assassinated on Christmas Day of 1942, Giraud succeeded him as supreme ruler of North Africa.

The situation in North Africa was ludicrous. Under Giraud a worse police terror than had existed under Darlan was unleashed. Anyone suspected of Gaullist sympathies was arrested and more than 50,000 were held in concentration camps. Giraud refused to repeal any of the Vichy legislation but did agree to declare the Vichy Constitution of 1940 null and void and reinstate the Constitution of 1875.

Eventually, under pressure from Roosevelt and Churchill, de Gaulle agreed to meet Giraud near Casablanca. De Gaulle had wanted to get together with Giraud several times in the past but not in the presence of Roosevelt and Churchill. He agreed to meet Giraud under the conditions created by Churchill and Roosevelt only reluctantly. Upon meeting Giraud, de Gaulle reprimanded him for not having joined the Free French after his escape from internment in Germany, and for his collaboration with the Vichyites. The meetings between the two men, which lasted several days, did not settle their major differences. Before leaving Casablanca, de Gaulle and Giraud met and prepared a communiqué. All it said was that the two men had met, discussed, and affirmed that the chief goal to be reached was the liberation of France, the triumph of human liberty, and the defeat of the enemy. It was nevertheless a friendly communiqué that left the door open for further negotiations on behalf of French unity. The two men concurred in the desirability of uniting and agreed to establish liaison between them to explore the possibility of achieving unity.[15]

Giraud was contributing to de Gaulle's strength by retaining his identification with Vichy, which was by then totally discredited. His most prominent followers were linked to Vichy as well. Although he ceased to act in the name of Vichy, he still accepted it as the source of his authority.[16]

By the late winter of 1943, General Giraud was becoming a source of embarrassment to the Americans and the British with his concentration camps and Vichy legislation. So General Catroux and Jean Monnet were sent to Algiers in an attempt to convert Giraud to the democratic faith. Within two months, Giraud had made enough concessions that de Gaulle again agreed to meet him face to face in order to settle the remaining differences.

The tireless efforts of intermediaries had brought the two generals closer to accord. At this second meeting the two men agreed to form a single government at Algiers. London was no longer the seat of government for the Free French, and the French National Committee in London was replaced by a new French Committee of National Liberation at Algiers. The latter was composed at first of only seven members with de Gaulle and Giraud as co-presidents.

The French Committee of National Liberation became a sort of provisional government of the French Republic and directed the French war effort everywhere. Its authority extended to all territories under the leadership of de Gaulle and Giraud. A consultative assembly under the committee emerged in September, 1943, composed of delegates appointed by all resistance groups including the Communists. Free France and the Resistance had been skillfully fused. As the year passed, the committee was increased from seven to fourteen and then to sixteen. De Gaulle's position within the committee was growing stronger while Giraud's star was rapidly dimming. Giraud was recognized as a great patriot and soldier who had succeeded in liberating Corsica from the Germans and the Italians, but as a political factor he had no policy, no skill, and no prestige.

He was eliminated as co-president of the Committee of National Liberation when, on September 25, 1943, de Gaulle proposed that the committee replace the system of the double presidency with a single, strong executive. Giraud protested, but the committee outvoted him. De Gaulle was appointed the sole president. Giraud remained commander in chief, but even in this position he was deprived of all but the most nominal powers over the army.

The following month de Gaulle claimed that it was necessary to reshape the ministries within the committee and asked all members of the committee to resign. Giraud was appalled when informed that his was one of the four resignations that had been accepted. The committee was then reorganized to include men handpicked by de Gaulle. Thus, five months after de Gaulle's arrival in Algiers, Giraud was eliminated as a factor in French affairs.

Free France and the Resistance movement had been merged, and by early 1944 the collaborators included merely a few hard-core, diehard reactionaries. The mass of citizens in metropolitan France awaited the liberation, which was now close at hand. Their hopes were enkindled by the Allied victories in North Africa, the invasion of Italy, and the Nazi defeat at Stalingrad.

Liberation and the Aftermath

On June 6, 1944, their hopes and dreams turned to reality. De Gaulle was, however, barred by Roosevelt from planning and executing the assault at Normandy. Therefore on D Day he was forced to remain in England. On June 13, de Gaulle and a small group of assistants went to Bayeux on the Normandy beachhead and made a visit that lasted several hours. By that time the National Liberation Committee had been officially renamed Provisional Government of the French Republic, and its authority was soon to be accepted by liberated France.

During the next two months, while France was being liberated by Anglo-American forces, de Gaulle received an audience with Pope Pius XII and then went on to Washington, D.C., for a meeting with FDR that did not go well. De Gaulle was convinced that Roosevelt wished to turn Western Europe into an American sphere of influence. However, no sooner did de Gaulle leave Washington and return to Algiers than he received a telegram from the State Department agreeing to recognize the French Committee of National Liberation (Provisional Government of the French Republic) as the provisional government of a liberated France. This recognition became official on October 23, 1944, one month after the government had been installed in Paris. By this time Roosevelt realized that de Gaulle's popularity was so overwhelming that he would be elected by a landslide in a free election.

On August 20, just before the liberation of Paris, an insurrection broke out in the city. De Gaulle was able to persuade Eisenhower that General Leclerc's armored division should be sent to Paris to enter the city first, and that the British and American forces would follow. Once Paris was captured by the Allies, de Gaulle entered the city before Eisenhower. He walked from the Etoile to the Hôtel de Ville to Notre Dame and was hailed by hundreds of thousands of Frenchmen as the symbol of French resistance, as the man who had never given up the ship.

Pétain and Laval were temporarily taken to Germany by the Nazi retreaters.

The Provisional Government of the French Republic under the leadership of General de Gaulle was in control. He ruled by consent. He became dictator until the completion of a new constitution but did not attempt to give himself unlimited powers. (De Gaulle resigned, however, before a constitution was completed by the Constituent Assembly, for reasons mentioned below.)

There were many political parties in France at the end of the war. Some were remnants of those that had existed during the Third Republic while others had been newly created during the occupation. All these parties had gone underground during the occupation. If de Gaulle had identified himself with any of these parties, its victory would have been guaranteed, but the General preferred to be a symbol, not a political leader.

During the short period in history between the liberation of France (1944) and January 20, 1946, the day de Gaulle resigned as leader of France, his emphasis was almost entirely on foreign policy. He sought alliances, not only with the United States and Great Britain, but with the USSR as well. De Gaulle believed that the political scene in Europe had not changed in the past seventy years and that Germany was still the primary threat. France immediately proved to be a very stubborn ally of the United States and Great Britain as soon as de Gaulle became her leader in 1944.

In December, 1944, de Gaulle journeyed to Moscow for a meeting with Stalin. Churchill advocated the signing of a new Anglo-Franco-Soviet alliance. De Gaulle did not favor a new Triple Entente because he was well aware that in such an arrangement, France would be the junior member. Instead, he proposed a Franco-Soviet alliance. He again told Stalin that Britain was not a continental power, did not understand land warfare, and that only France and the USSR, the two largest European powers, could hold Germany in check in the future. At this point, Stalin tried a diplomatic coup. He would agree to a strictly Franco-Soviet alliance if de Gaulle would recognize the Lublin Committee (composed almost entirely of Polish Communists) as the new provisional government of Poland. Both the United States and Great Britain refused to recognize this committee as the legitimate representative of post-World War II Poland. De Gaulle became offended at this suggestion and left the Kremlin abruptly.

But he was brought back within a short time, and Stalin gave way, signing an alliance with France that did not include Britain. (De Gaulle had also tried to obtain Stalin's recognition of the Rhine River as France's eastern boundary. Stalin refused unless the United States and Great Britain would also agree.)

But he was brought back within a short time, and Stalin gave way, signing an alliance with France that did not include Britain.

The General's stubbornness toward the end of the war undoubtedly stemmed from his determination to be treated as the leader of a great power. He refused to meet President Roosevelt at Algiers on his return from the Yalta Conference in February, 1945, because of his resentment at having been excluded from the conference. It was again Roosevelt, not Stalin, who insisted that de Gaulle be excluded. Neither was de Gaulle invited to the Potsdam Conference in the summer of 1945. France had planned to oppose the United Nations Charter but dropped her opposition upon being informed that she would be a permanent member of the Security Council with the power to veto any resolution.[17]

With de Gaulle firmly in power, the United States and Great Britain carved out of their own zones of occupation in Germany a zone for France, and the latter took her seat on the Allied Control Council for Germany.

At first, the USSR welcomed French participation on the council, since the Kremlin saw France as a three-time victim of German aggression within seventy years and an old ally of Russia as well. The Soviet Union hoped that France would side with her and compel the United States and Great Britain to impose a harsh peace on defeated Germany.

De Gaulle wanted to become mediator between East and West, between the United States and Great Britain on the one hand and the USSR on the other. France's new alliance with the USSR, which was signed on December 9, 1944, had already been ratified by both countries by February 15, 1945. But on January 20, 1946, de Gaulle resigned as the leader of France over the failure of the Constituent Assembly to draft a constitution giving the chief executive strong power and over its failure to appropriate money sufficient enough to allow de Gaulle to build up a strong military force.

France's effort to mediate between East and West continued to manifest itself for a short time after de Gaulle's resignation, and in the spring of 1946 France voted more than once on the Security Council with the USSR against the United States and Great Britain.

The new French government did not differ from de Gaulle in regarding Germany as Enemy Number One. In early 1947, after the new French constitution creating a Fourth Republic had been accepted, France proposed a plan for separating the Rhineland from the remainder of Germany and advocated a four-power supervision of the Ruhr. Hoping to weaken Germany and expecting that the Russians would jump at this opportunity to gain a foothold in the West, France miscalculated. At the meeting in Moscow of the Council of Foreign Ministers, the USSR as well as the United States and Great Britain rejected the plan. The USSR apparently felt that she had nothing to gain in that the three Western powers would outvote her in the Ruhr. Besides, the Soviet Union had little to gain at this point in history by supporting the French government domestically or internationally.[18] The USSR began to denounce France as well as Great Britain as a colonial power, and instead supported the French Communists, who were beginning to go into opposition against the government.

The Paris Conference of July, 1947, over the Marshall Plan and Soviet refusal to allow her satellites to accept this aid proved that Europe was divided into two parts. It was becoming apparent that France was neither strong enough to mediate between East and West nor to induce the United States and Great Britain to maintain a hard line on Germany. France was forced to choose between the USSR, which was threatening all of Europe, and the United States and Great Britain, who wished to strengthen Germany.

With the Communist takeover of Czechoslovakia, France realized that times had indeed changed and that the major threat came not from Germany but from Communist Russia. By 1948, France reluctantly agreed to the Anglo-American plan, which called for the merger of the three Western zones of Germany and the establishment of the Federal Republic of Germany, in which the West Germans would have a major say in deciding its form. Between 1950 and 1955 France gave in, inch by inch, to the rearmament of West Germany.

From all outward appearances, it seemed that France had become a bona fide ally, a rank and file member of the Atlantic Alliance. But it was during this period (1946-1958) that French foreign policy deviated from the past, and with the subsequent return of Charles de Gaulle to power, France embarked on her traditional policy of establishing hegemony over Western and Central Europe and a détente with the Soviet Union and her new satellites in Eastern Europe.

CHAPTER 2

De Gaulle Returns to Power

C HARLES de Gaulle resigned as leader of France on January 20, 1946, because the Constituent Assembly seemed to be drafting a constitution that provided for a strong legislative branch and a weak executive. De Gaulle was a champion of strong executive leadership. The Third Republic (1871-1940), which provided for a parliamentary system of government and a president who amounted to a ceremonial leader, was characterized by numerous cabinet crises because the various political parties could not agree on even the most basic issues. Rarely did a political party poll more than 50 percent of the votes and therefore most governments were coalition governments during this period. De Gaulle did not wish to return to a system similar to that of the Third Republic. Nevertheless, a constitution similar to the Constitution of the Third Republic was drafted, creating a Fourth Republic of France.

The period between 1946 and 1958 was even more unstable than the period of the Third Republic. There were numerous political parties and constant changes of government. The brief life of every cabinet, the uncertainty of its support in parliament, and the necessity for compromise between widely different points of view allowed for little continuity of policy.

To make things even worse, deputies in the National Assembly took pleasure in plotting and counterplotting and in the thrill of bringing down a government. Perhaps in ordinary times this game could have been tolerated, but these were not ordinary times.[1] There were a series of crises in the 1950's: the Cold War, the Indochina fiasco, the Suez crisis, and finally Algeria. The Fourth Republic had succeeded in alienating a large majority of the French people and in driving others into apathy.

The Algerian War was the last crisis of the Fourth Republic. Supported by patriotic right-wing organizations, the army refused to obey the last government of the Fourth Republic. Gaullist groups, fearing a military coup, called for the return of General de Gaulle, who expressed his willingness to resume power. This was the opportunity for which he had waited twelve years. On June 1, 1958, the National Assembly elected de Gaulle prime minister. He formed a cabinet, and the following day the Constitution of the Fourth Republic was amended empowering de Gaulle to draft a new constitution. Thus, the Fourth Republic came to an end several months later when the Constitution of the Fifth Republic was completed and approved by the French people.

Under the Constitution of 1958, the greatly increased executive power centers on the president of the Republic, who is elected for seven years and is capable of giving stability to French political life. However, the constitution does not give France solely a presidential regime. There is also a prime minister and a cabinet who are responsible to the National Assembly, which can overthrow the government but not the president.

The Constitution of 1958 is a monarchical constitution in republican disguise. The president acts as a constitutional monarch but exercises considerable power, as did King Louis Philippe of France between 1830 and 1848. Under such a system, the king or president guarantees the stability of the government of the country. He rules, but leaves the day-to-day matters to the cabinet. But he steps in and decides with finality if a crisis arises.[2] The Constitution of 1958 gave the president of France absolute power in terms of making foreign policy, which was Charles de Gaulle's first and foremost priority.

The General realized, however, that he could not even begin to think about foreign policy and his "Grand Design" of détente, entente, and building one Europe from the Atlantic to the Urals, which he had espoused since the end of World War II, until he solved the domestic problems of France, which included the problems of Black Africa and Algeria. Although one can discern between the return of de Gaulle to power and the independence of Algeria in 1962 a foreign policy that differed from that of the Fourth Republic, it was not until the independence of Algeria that de Gaulle began to concentrate almost totally on foreign policy and to build a new policy that distinguished France from other Western nations.

During the period of the Fourth Republic, the problems that France had been experiencing over the previous fifty or more years simply became magnified. In the industrial realm, France was not increasing at a rate of production anywhere near that of her neighbors. The population problem continued, and during certain years, deaths outnumbered births. The nation was divided by political, social, and religious struggles, and the Algerian crisis that followed the humiliating defeat in Indochina brought France to the brink of civil war. In the midst of all of these problems, Black Africa, including the French territories, was stirring. French credit was exhausted, the currency was ruined, and inflation was running wild.

The French people realized at long last that their country was heading toward disaster and that the Fourth Republic with its numerous political parties, which, in many instances, represented nothing but small factions, could no longer be permitted to govern in the present manner. France then turned to strong leadership in the person of Charles de Gaulle. Within a short time after his return to power, most of these problems were at least under control.

The Economy

During the period between June 1, 1958, when he became last premier of the Fourth Republic, and January 8, 1959, when he became president of the Fifth Republic following the popular referendum approving the new constitution, de Gaulle ruled with emergency powers.

De Gaulle conferred upon the country new institutions adapted to the requirements of a modern democracy and brought about fundamental political reforms necessary for a profound and lasting economic recovery.

During this period of emergency, he undertook stern measures in the economic realm. Salaries of personnel working in public concerns, including government workers and military personnel, were frozen as were salaries of people working with private concerns during the emergency. One hundred and nineteen millions in additional taxes were imposed on people in the higher income bracket. Between May and August, 1958, the balance of trade deficit dropped from $178.6 million to $119.1 million.[3]

At the same time, a drive was under way to rebuild all facets of the economy. Agricultural and industrial production were increased and the highway system, railroads, ports, airports, and water supply improved.

De Gaulle was forced to choose one of two alternatives: (1) a planned economy in the form of rigorous freezing of prices and wages, a drastic curtailment of social security benefits, and a massive creation of new taxes, all in order to safeguard an unrealistic monetary parity; or (2) freedom of production and trade at the cost of a moderate devaluation of the franc. The second path was chosen.

The first budgetary estimates for 1959 showed a net treasury deficit double that of 1958 (1,180 billion old francs as against 600 billion in 1958).[4] On the world market, France was pricing herself out of her export markets. This factor combined with inflation at home threatened to increase the already considerable deficit.

The remedies selected to rectify the situation were increased investments at home, a balanced budget, and the devaluation of the franc. The total funds earmarked for public capital expenditures rose from 1,124 billion old francs in 1958 to 1,470 billion in 1959, an increase of 25 percent in the state budget.[5]

The chief aims were to bring the budgetary deficit down to a safer level and to create through fiscal reform the conditions proper for a stable economic growth. A liberalization in trade was undertaken. The franc was devalued by 17 percent and at the same time it was made fully convertible into any other currency. Convertibility of the franc was supplemented by a series of measures to encourage foreign investment in France.

Economic expansion, which constituted the chief objective of the government's policy, was already showing marked improvement by the end of 1959 through capital investment. This expansion was also stimulated as a result of the more realistic rate of exchange of the franc and its convertibility.

On January 1, 1959, the old-age pension was increased by fifty new francs per month.[6] Through cooperation between employers and organized labor, a special fund was created. Designed to maintain employment, this fund assured unemployed workers of an additional payment bringing their benefits almost up to the level of the minimum wage. As for personnel employed directly by the state in the civil service, the public services, and nationalized enterprises, beginning February 1, 1959, their remuneration was increased by 4 percent.[7]

All of these reforms worked extremely well. Because of the new reforms, the devaluation of 17 percent was accompanied by a price rise of less than 7 percent in 1959, whereas every other devaluation in the past had been accompanied by a massive increase in prices and an upset in the balance of trade.

By the time Algeria became independent in July, 1962, France was again a prosperous country with a strong economy. Never before, to use de Gaulle's own words, had there been so much production, construction, and instruction. Never before had the standard of living been so high. Never before had France had so little unemployment. Never before had the French currency been stronger. Instead of borrowing, France was beginning to make loans to other countries. In that same year (1962) de Gaulle implemented a new plan which was to increase the power and prosperity of France almost 25 percent within the next four years.[8]

Within two years from the time de Gaulle returned to power, the birthrate made a striking comeback and births began to outnumber deaths by 300,000 per year. The attitude of the nation reflected a feeling of optimism for the first time since the end of World War II.

The French Community

French Black Africa was stirring before de Gaulle returned to power. Soon after his return, he announced that a community would be formed between France and her overseas territories that desired to belong. In the referendum provided by the Constitution of the Fifth Republic of France, the overseas territories were offered four choices: immediate independence; the status of Overseas Departments of France with representation in the French parliament; the status quo, which would mean retention of their position as overseas Territories; or the opportunity to join a new association known as the French Community. Even after becoming a member of the community, a state could eventually choose to assume its own destiny independently of the others after coming to an agreement with the organs of the community.

Eleven of the former colonial territories in French West and Equatorial Africa and the island of Madagascar voted to join the new community, and, in early 1959, each adopted a constitution, elected a legislature, and formed its own government. Only Guinea voted to sever all ties with France.

Each member of the French Community became internally self-governing, while foreign affairs, defense, and economic and financial policy came under the jurisdiction of the community as a whole. Executive authority within the community was vested in the president of the French Republic and an executive council composed of the premiers of all member states. A senate and a court of arbitration were also included as organs of the community.

Despite the changed political status of the former territories, France acknowledged a continuing responsibility for aiding the economic development of these less-advanced areas.

The community set up by the Constitution of the Fifth Republic underwent important changes in 1960. Following the May 18, 1960, amendment to the Constitution of the Fifth Republic, a member state could become independent and still continue to belong to the community. All eleven African states and the Malagasy Republic (formerly Madagascar) chose to become independent in 1960. Six decided to remain in the "remodeled" French Community, while the other six preferred to retain bilateral ties with France outside the community.

Algeria

Political life in France was dominated by the Algerian problem during the first three and a half years of de Gaulle's presidency. Algeria was by far the most serious of all the problems that confronted de Gaulle, and it nearly led to his downfall. Several attempts were made on his life because of the Algerian problem, and it was a miracle that he escaped every one.

When de Gaulle assumed the role of last premier of the Fourth Republic, he announced that there would be no negotiations with the Algerian rebels. At the same time he offered them peace with honor. As a champion of nationalism, de Gaulle was well aware that the Algerian people were struggling for their national identity, and he had every intention of giving these people the right to self-determination in due time. As time passed, any doubts that de Gaulle had once had with regard to how the Algerian Moslems would vote if given the free choice became clarified in his mind. He was convinced that France must leave Algeria voluntarily or she would be forced out. But de Gaulle would agree to France's leaving Algeria only at a time when peace, order, and

stability could be restored to the country and maintained thereaf-
ter.

On September 16, 1959, de Gaulle in a nationwide radio-
television broadcast announced that the Algerian people should
have the right to determine their own future. He offered the
rebel leaders an immediate peace. Once pacification had been
achieved, there would be a four-year period of transition. At the
end of four years, the Algerian people would be given one of
three choices: remain an Overseas Department of France; become a member of the newly established French Community;
gain complete independence from France.[9]

Since de Gaulle was not in favor of the status quo in Algeria on
the one hand and associated Algerian independence with political
instability on the other, he was hoping that the Algerian people
would vote to enter the French Community. In 1960, when all of
the members of the community voted to become independent,
some deciding to remain part of the "remodeled" French Community and others deciding to maintain bilateral relations with
France outside the community, de Gaulle hoped that Algeria
would follow one of these two paths in the future.

De Gaulle's proposal to grant the Algerian people the right to
self-determination was received with a storm of protest by the
European minority (overwhelmingly French) in Algeria, known as
"the Ultras." They accused de Gaulle of treason for making such
a suggestion, even though the vast majority of Frenchmen in
metropolitan France favored this plan.

Many Frenchmen believed that the army would never abide by
de Gaulle's decision to allow the Algerian people the right to
self-determination. January 24, 1960, the Ultras began mass demonstrations against de Gaulle in Algiers. The spark that led to
the demonstration was de Gaulle's dismissal of General Massau,
one of his generals in Algeria, for making public statements
criticizing de Gaulle's self-determination proposal.[10] When the
French police ordered the demonstrators to disperse, they were
fired upon. Several gendarmes were killed and many others
wounded. The commander in chief then declared a state of siege
in Algiers, and additional troops were rushed to the city.
Massau's paratroops were withdrawn from Algeria and replaced
by those loyal to the French government. A number of suspected
Ultras were rounded up and arrested and there was a purge

within the army. In France itself, public opinion favored de Gaulle even more than it had before the insurrection in Algiers because the French people were impressed with the manner in which de Gaulle had handled himself during this crisis.

In his address on Algerian policy, broadcast over French radio and television on January 29, 1960, de Gaulle tried to appease both the Ultras and the army. He tried to leave the Ultras with the impression that their honor was not at stake and that the new Algeria would be closely identified with France. He told the army that it must liquidate the rebel force (National Liberation Front, known as FLN) that was seeking to drive France out of Algeria and at the same time was attempting to impose a dictatorship of want and sterility on the Algerian people. De Gaulle said that when it came time for the Algerians to vote, it would be the duty of the army to guarantee the complete freedom and responsibility of the vote.[11]

In the press conference of September 5, 1960, de Gaulle said that there is an Algeria, there is an Algerian entity, there is an Algerian personality, and it is up to the Algerians to decide their own destiny by their vote.[12] Two months later, in a nationwide broadcast, he announced that he was following a new course in Algeria leading to an Algeria governed by the Algerians, not by metropolitan France. He suggested setting up provisional new institutions in Algeria even before the final vote on self-determination, but remained adamant in his refusal to recognize the provisional government.

In his annual New Year's address to the French people on December 31, 1960, de Gaulle again tried to appease the Ultras by telling them that Algeria needed the French Community after her independence. No matter what happened he declared, France would protect her children, whatever their origins, in their persons and in their property, just as she would safeguard her own interests.

One week later, he asked the peoples of France and Algeria to vote yes in the referendum that would be held in both nations on January 8, 1961. Although the wording of the referendum was vague, de Gaulle was asking for an approval of his policy in Algeria. Metropolitan France voted 3 to 1 in favor. In Algeria the FLN asked the Algerian Moslems to boycott the election but many, nevertheless, did vote, and those who did, voted yes. Almost all of the Europeans in Algeria voted, and they voted overwhelmingly no. The final vote in Algeria was 1,700,000 yes and 700,000 no.

This referendum, which was held only sixteen months after de Gaulle had first announced his decision to allow the people of Algeria the right to self-determination four years after the achievement of pacification, represented a softening in his original position. The explanation seems to be simple enough. Shortly after de Gaulle's nationwide radio-television broadcast of September 16, 1959, in which he announced his decision on self-determination in Algeria, all of the nations of the French Community voted in favor of independence. In addition, Morocco and Tunisia, neighbors of Algeria, had achieved their independence. De Gaulle realized at this point that he would have to move up considerably the date he had originally had in mind for a vote on self-determination.

The final vote on Algerian self-determination would have taken place even before July 1, 1962; but soon after the referendum of January 8, 1961, which went overwhelmingly in favor of de Gaulle, four generals, Challe, Salan, Jouhaud, and Zeller, who had recently resigned from the army, staged a putsch in Algiers. The High Command in Algeria announced a state of siege. The question hinged on whether the army both in France and in Algeria would follow these new insurgents.

De Gaulle acted swiftly. Members of the army suspected of sympathizing with the insurgents were arrested and a financial and economic blockade was set up against Algeria. De Gaulle assumed emergency dictatorial powers under Article 16 of the constitution.

On April 23, de Gaulle made another nationwide broadcast condemning the actions of the four retired generals supported by fanatic officers who were leading France toward disaster. Many rank-and-file French soldiers in Algeria as well as officers listened to this speech and vowed to resist the four generals. All of France except the extreme right was behind de Gaulle and likened the French generals to the Vichyite fascist traitors. One of the four, General Challe, surrendered, while the other three, Salan, Jouhaud, and Zeller went into hiding. Numerous arrests followed and regiments in Algeria guilty of rebellion were disbanded.

The trouble was far from over. The O.A.S. (Organisation de l'Armée Secrète), a right-wing terrorist organization, was angered by the failure of the putsch and intensified its terrorism both in France and in Algeria, and the FLN increased its terrorism as well.

At this point the O.A.S. made an all-out attempt to assassinate de Gaulle. On September 8, 1961, he barely escaped assassination when his car was blown up on the road from Paris to his home in Colombey-les-Deux-Eglises. The O.A.S. announced that the assassination of de Gaulle was the last hope of saving French Algeria. De Gaulle was even more determined than ever that the Algerian affair be settled by the end of 1962 and that the French army be brought back to metropolitan France.

On March 18, 1962, an agreement was signed between Charles de Gaulle and Ben Khedda, prime minister of the provisional government of Algeria, at Evian. According to the Evian Agreement, after the referendum on self-determination in Algeria, Europeans could, if they wished, remain in Algeria and become either Algerian citizens or privileged foreigners. A referendum was held in France on April 8, 1962, asking the people whether or not they wished to give President de Gaulle freedom to draw up laws on the basis of the Evian Agreement. More than 90 percent voted yes. Only the far right, which sympathized with the O.A.S., voted no.[13]

Many of the Ultras had already seen the handwriting on the wall and began to leave Algeria for France in droves. Their pessimism was heightened by the arrests of General Jouhaud, a ranking official of the O.A.S., on March 25 and General Salan on April 20. In spite of all these events, terrorism on the part of the O.A.S. increased in the months following while Europeans, fearing for their lives, continued to leave Algeria.

When the referendum on self-determination for the Algerian people was held on July 1, 1962, nearly half the Europeans had already left Algeria, and most of those that remained did not even bother to participate in the vote. The result of the election was that 99 percent of those who participated voted in favor of an Algeria fully independent from France, and on July 3, 1962, Algerian independence was proclaimed.

With the Algerian problem behind him, de Gaulle could now turn to his most important task of developing a coherent foreign policy, which would soon distinguish his country from the other nations of Western Europe.

CHAPTER 3

De Gaulle and the West

A FTER de Gaulle returned to power in 1958, it soon became apparent to many political analysts that he was pursuing a foreign policy that differed from that of the Fourth Republic. As early as September, 1958, when he was still the last prime minister of the Fourth Republic, he came out in favor of a global strategy for NATO. De Gaulle said that American preponderance in NATO was too great and that the recent affair in Lebanon as well as the Quemoy-Matsu crisis had shown that there existed a lack of coordination among the allies.[1] He felt that, as things stood, the United States was able to take independent action in parts of the world not covered by NATO, yet endanger the peace in so doing. In addition, the United States was free to decide on the use of nuclear weapons without consulting her allies.

In an attempt to remedy this situation, de Gaulle wrote letters to President Eisenhower and Prime Minister Macmillan on September 24, 1958, suggesting that a tridirectorate within NATO composed of the United States, Great Britain, and France be formed to coordinate global strategy. Political analysts have speculated as to de Gaulle's motives in making such a proposal. Is it sufficient to say that this was a strange proposal coming from a man who would within such a short time denounce the division of the world into two power blocs?

De Gaulle's plan for the so-called tridirectorate within NATO would have amounted to putting the free world under a three-nation bloc. West Germany, Italy, and Belgium vehemently objected. The suggestion met with little response from Washington too, since the United States did not think much of France as a military power. At first, the United States underestimated not only the stubbornness of Charles de Gaulle but his independence of mind as well. Once Washington became convinced that de Gaulle was pursuing a foreign policy that was not in the interest of the United States, it attempted to buy him off by making proposals similar to that of the tridirectorate, each intended to put France on an equal plane with Great Britain as an ally of the United States.

Several writers feel that the plan for a tridirectorate was merely a tactic of de Gaulle, not a sincere proposal. One anti-Gaullist writer goes so far as to assert that de Gaulle knew that neither the United States nor other NATO countries would accept his tridirectorate to coordinate global strategy outside Europe. Consequently, the author continues, he used this knowledge as an excuse to withdraw the French Mediterranean fleet from the Allied High Command in NATO, because the area south of the Mediterranean was not covered by NATO and de Gaulle could argue that France might one day have to use this fleet to defend Algeria and members of the French Community in Africa. Moreover, this same writer points out that the French fleet within NATO was French controlled and in a time of peace could be used as de Gaulle saw fit. In case of trouble in an isolated part of the world like Algeria or the French Community, de Gaulle could use the French Mediterranean fleet to defend those areas even though the fleet was part of NATO. The writer is actually saying that de Gaulle's true purpose in withdrawing the French Mediterranean fleet from NATO was to de-earmark it in the event of war, so that it could be used as France wished.[2]

De Gaulle's proposal of a tridirectorate and his withdrawal of the French Mediterranean fleet from NATO can, however, be viewed in a different light. When de Gaulle was asked about the withdrawal of this fleet from NATO at his first press conference as president of France on March 25, 1959, he not only mentioned that the Middle East, North Africa, Black Africa, and the Red Sea were not covered by NATO and that France might one day need her Mediterranean fleet to take independent action in that part of the world but also pointed out that the other two great world powers of the Atlantic Alliance, the United States and Great Britain, had taken steps to prevent the greater part of their naval forces from being integrated into NATO. Perhaps de Gaulle's proposal of a tridirectorate within NATO to coordinate global strategy was sincere. Since France was the only one of the three located in continental Europe, the other two, by accepting the tridirectorate, would be recognizing French predominance in Europe. His withdrawal of the French Mediterranean fleet from NATO may not have been prompted by the refusal of Great Britain and the United States to accept the proposal of the tridirectorate. It may well have been prompted by the fact that the majority of the American and British naval forces were free to act independently from NATO, and, therefore, de Gaulle felt that a large portion of the French fleet should have the same independence of action.

De Gaulle, in the same press conference, went on to say: "I believe that the Alliance will be all the more vital and strong as the great powers unite on the basis of cooperation in which each carries his own load, rather than on the basis of an integration in which peoples and governments find themselves more and more deprived of their roles and responsibilities in the domain of their own defense."[3] De Gaulle was already asserting his opposition to integration of forces and his belief that the defense of each country should have a national character.

When de Gaulle came to power, the Eisenhower administration offered him a privileged status. If he had chosen, de Gaulle could have built up an association with the United States that would in time have surpassed that of Great Britain, whose special relationship with Washington was beginning to lag by the late 1950's, reflecting Britain's declining position in the world. If de Gaulle had wished, he could have made France the privileged partner of the United States. But the United States simply could not offer de Gaulle anything that he wanted except the right to share nuclear secrets with the American government, for which he was not willing to pay a political price. De Gaulle had no desire for France to replace Great Britain as the junior partner of the United States or to strengthen France's links with the United States. His desire was to detach Europe from the United States.[4]

President Eisenhower's Attempts
to Woo de Gaulle

Eisenhower was in favor of assisting de Gaulle's nuclear program with no strings attached. Perhaps as a retired general himself, he felt an admiration, even a warmth, for de Gaulle. He may even have felt that in offering France nuclear assistance, he could persuade de Gaulle to take a more moderate line. It was the Atomic Energy Committee's opposition that prevented Eisenhower from assisting de Gaulle's nuclear program. Under the Atomic Energy Act, the President of the United States was obliged to obtain final approval from the Atomic Energy Committee before giving such assistance to a foreign nation, and the committee did not approve of de Gaulle's attitude toward NATO.

During the last two years of the Eisenhower presidency, Secretary of State Dulles had several meetings with de Gaulle. At their last meeting in the winter of 1959, when Dulles was already gravely ill, he was instructed by President Eisenhower to hold out the possibility of a French veto on American nuclear weapons deployed in continental Europe, an offer that had never been made to Great Britain. The words "advanced authorization" were used in place of the word "veto," but an advanced authorization amounted to a veto. De Gaulle's failure to respond may have been motivated by one of three considerations: he may have failed to grasp the significance of what the United States was offering him; he may have been so astonished by this offer that he could not find the words to reply; he may not have wanted what was being offered to him.

The third was the most likely. De Gaulle was being offered what amounted to a partnership with the United States, and he did not wish to be a partner but rather an independent ally. Since his ultimate goal was total withdrawal of U.S. forces from Europe (in the distant future), he would have had to revise his policy completely if he had accepted this offer. It was not worth the offer for de Gaulle to swallow his pride, revise his policy, and stop speaking about American hegemony in Western Europe, when, if successful, his own policy would result in an end to American hegemony and in a Western Europe that would accept the political leadership of France.

At his second press conference on November 10, 1959, de Gaulle defended the right of his country to test atomic weapons in the Sahara after such tests had been suspended by the United States, Great Britain, and the USSR. He said that after World War II, the United States was the only atomic power. In 1946, she offered to turn over all her nuclear weapons to the United Nations Organization on the condition that no other nation seek to have such weapons for itself. The USSR refused the offer, wishing to manufacture them for herself. As a result, Great Britain followed suit, and today the three could destroy all life on this planet many times over. Finally, after having acquired a knowledge that enabled them to perfect their nuclear weapons, the three powers suspended their tests before France had an opportunity to begin hers. De Gaulle expressed his annoyance that the UN neither condemned the manufacture of nuclear weapons by these three powers nor asked them to destroy such weapons. He resented the emotionalism then being expressed at the UN against France for testing atomic weapons, and said that he could not regard it as anything but an arbitrary maneuver against his country.

In truth, he felt that France was rendering a service to the equilibrium of the world by equipping herself with nuclear armaments. De Gaulle urged the UN to make an attempt to place under international control the use of rockets, which he called the vehicles of death. If the UN succeeded in this endeavor, which would represent a big step toward total disarmament, France would conform to such an agreement without hesitation.[5]

De Gaulle Reaffirms Loyalty
to the Atlantic Alliance

Shortly after de Gaulle's second press conference, at which he lashed out against the arbitrary move against France in the UN for her testing of atomic weapons, he reaffirmed his loyalty to the Atlantic Alliance.

In speaking before the Foreign Affairs Committee of the National Assembly, Foreign Minister Couve de Murville, who spoke in the name of de Gaulle, said that the Atlantic Alliance was necessary and would continue to remain necessary until a real peace had been established. He stressed France's loyalty to the alliance and claimed that even though she had withdrawn her Mediterranean fleet from NATO because these naval units might be necessary to defend nations not covered by the Atlantic Alliance, this fleet would take part in the Battle of the Mediterranean if the time should ever come. However, the proposal to pool all equipment and place the entire air defenses in Europe under a single command smacked of integration and was not well received by de Gaulle. He felt it unwise to give to a commander in chief who was not directly under orders from the French government the right to open fire on the enemy from French soil.[6]

At the same time, the American government requested from

the French government an authorization to set up at several points on French soil depots of nuclear bombs that would be used if necessary to arm certain American aviation units stationed in France. De Gaulle did not agree to this request, since it too raised the question of unleashing a nuclear war.[7]

De Gaulle spoke with Prime Minister Macmillan on numerous occasions between 1958 and 1963. Their first meeting took place in June, 1958, only days after de Gaulle became the last prime minister of the Fourth Republic. The General was already complaining about NATO as it existed and felt that it needed a global strategy. This was also the first occasion on which de Gaulle proposed the tridirectorate within NATO. The two men spoke at length about Algeria, but little time was devoted to Franco-British relations and European problems.

During de Gaulle's visit to London in March, 1960, just before his visit to the United States, Macmillan informed de Gaulle that Great Britain did not wish to join the Common Market at that time.[8] De Gaulle was a man who thought in long-range terms and he believed even during his visit to London in 1960 that Britain would one day enter Europe through membership in the Common Market. Within one year, Macmillan would change his mind and Britain would apply for membership.

When de Gaulle visited the United States in the spring of 1960, after having visited Great Britain, he received a warmer welcome from the American people than had any other statesman in recent history. France had already made her first atomic test in the Sahara. Although President Eisenhower wanted to share American data in the nuclear field with France, as he was doing with Great Britain, the Joint Atomic Energy Committee and its allies within the Department of State were doing their best to block this endeavor, distrusting de Gaulle because of his attitude toward NATO.

Although his address before a joint session of Congress was received with overwhelming applause, his most revealing comment during the entire trip came at the National Press Club in Washington, D.C. When asked about the USSR, de Gaulle stated, as he had already said in his *Mémoires*, that France and Russia were natural allies and that between the two countries there was no conflict of interest. Even though de Gaulle was taking a hard line on the Berlin crisis, he was letting it be known that his long-range policy had an Eastern orientation. This comment went over the heads of most political observers but should have been sufficient to put the United States on notice.

Press Conference of September 5, 1960

De Gaulle stressed the importance of building and uniting Europe at his third press conference. He drew a distinction between "following our dreams and proceeding in accordance with realities" in undertaking this most important endeavor. De Gaulle would, at a later time, spell out in detail his plan for the political unification of Europe, but he did make it quite clear in this press conference that a supranational Europe, which some members of the Common Market were already advocating, was a dream devoid of all reality since each nation had its own spirit, history, language, culture, and traditions that differed from those of the others.[9]

When questioned about NATO, he said that at the time the Atlantic Alliance was organized, the United States was the only nation that had the means to defend Western Europe, and for this reason the alliance was organized on the basis of integration, a system of defense in which the nations of Western Europe did not have a national character. With the exception of the British forces, which were not integrated with those of the other members of the alliance, everything was under the command of the United States, which decided on the use of all weapons.

However, de Gaulle continued, within a short time after the organization of the alliance, it became evident that there was a possibility that a conflict could develop outside Europe, and there arose among the members of the Atlantic Alliance differences concerning strategy. Then, as time passed, the nations of Western Europe got back on their feet and regained their national identity. De Gaulle believed that the changes that had come about in the world necessitated two changes in NATO. First, he repeated that the organization needed a global strategy. He said that if the three powers of the Atlantic Alliance could not agree on matters other than those that concerned Europe, the alliance would not be indefinitely maintained even in Europe. Second, since the nations of Europe had regained their national identities, the defense of each country should have its own national character. Furthermore, if atomic weapons were to be stockpiled on

French territory, these weapons must be under the command of French forces. France could not leave her destiny to the direction of others. Thus, de Gaulle was merely defining in more detail ideas that he had already formulated on the major issues concerning Europe since his return to power.

De Gaulle's reserved attitude toward the United Nations, which he felt had treated France unfairly during the atomic tests in the Sahara, manifested itself in full at his press conference of April 11, 1961. He explained that France was one of the charter members of the United Nations. When that organization was founded in 1945, it was composed of the Security Council, a sort of government that included the Big Five, and a nonlegislative deliberative parliament, the General Assembly. The latter was supposed to debate only subjects submitted to it by the Security Council and included only about forty states that had been in existence for many years, endowed with cohesion and unity and used to international relations with its traditions, obligations, and responsibilities. In the Security Council, each of the big powers had the right to veto any substantive resolution, and in the General Assembly, a two-thirds majority was necessary to pass such a resolution. The charter forbade intervention by the organization into the internal affairs of states except upon specific request of the government of the state involved.

De Gaulle suggested that the United Nations no longer resembled what it was in 1945, nor what it ought to have been from the start. The Security Council consisted not only of the Big Five but also of several powers elected in turn. The General Assembly had assumed all powers and could deliberate on anything without the advice of the Security Council, which had been dispossessed of its essential function. In addition, the General Assembly included more than one hundred states and its number was climbing each year.

Since the charter inconvenienced everyone, nobody could enforce it. Even minimal cooperation between East and West in the UN did not exist, and the meetings had become in de Gaulle's own words "no more than riotous and scandalous sessions where there is no way to organize an objective debate and which are filled with invectives and insults thrown out, especially by the communists and those who are allied with them against the Western nations."[10]

Under these conditions, de Gaulle stressed that the French attitude toward the UN could only be one of reserve. He would not agree to contribute men and money to any present or future undertaking of the organization until reason and common sense began to prevail among the members. Throughout his entire presidency, de Gaulle's attitude toward the UN did not change significantly.

De Gaulle again protested against the outcry of indignation hurled upon France by the UN for conducting three atomic tests in the Sahara as opposed to 120 tests conducted by the United States, Great Britain, and the USSR. His negative attitude toward the UN was without doubt conditioned, at least in part, by the organization's attitude toward the conduct of nuclear tests by France. De Gaulle claimed that the three powers were no longer testing these weapons because they had no need for further tests. The three still possessed stockpiles capable of annihilating the world, and none of the three had agreed to destroy these stockpiles. The race among them merely moved into the area of building missiles for launching bombs.

De Gaulle, Kennedy, and Macmillan

John F. Kennedy visited Paris in the spring of 1961 while en route to Vienna for a meeting with Khrushchev. In a series of meetings with de Gaulle between May 31 and June 2 the two men agreed on little except for Berlin, but the meetings at least served to produce rapport between them. De Gaulle was unimpressed with Khrushchev's threats over Berlin. What he did fear was that the Berlin crisis would serve to draw the United States and the USSR close together bilaterally and that this closeness would conflict with his own long-range plans.

It was Kennedy who helped to convince Macmillan that the Common Market was a greater success than anybody could have imagined three years earlier and that it would be in the interest of Britain to join. Two months after Kennedy's meeting with de Gaulle, Great Britain applied for admission to the Common Market.

At his press conference of September 5, 1961, de Gaulle said that ever since the creation of the Common Market the Six had wanted other nations, particularly Great Britain, to join. But the problem was complex, he added, since every member must assume the obligations involved as well as the advantages that accrued from membership. De Gaulle continued to waver through-out 1962 with regard to British membership in the Common Market. Before the final settlement of the Algerian Affair, he was more optimistic than pessimistic in his statements about British membership, but after Algeria became independent in the sum-mer of 1962 his statements on membership reflected pessimism.

Gaullist writers are not in agreement about de Gaulle's true feelings vis-à-vis British membership in the Common Market. Some assert that de Gaulle knew all along that he would veto a motion for British membership if all went well for him in Algeria. He had to proceed with caution on this subject before the final vote on Algerian independence, since his political position in France was shaky and he could not afford to antagonize the other five members of the Common Market, who all favored British participation. Once the Algerian question was settled, he had a freer hand in the matter.

Other Gaullist writers claim that de Gaulle was not playing a devious game and assert that only when he became convinced that Britain wanted all the benefits of membership and few of the obligations did he decide to veto Britain's bid. The story is, how-ever, more complex than either of these two explanations.

Macmillan met de Gaulle twice in 1962 in order to discuss British participation in the Common Market with him. Both times Macmillan journeyed to France for the meetings. In June, 1962, he visited de Gaulle at the Château de Champs. After the meeting, de Gaulle expressed optimism about British member-ship in the European Economic Community (EEC). But between their meeting at the Château de Champs and their meeting at Rambouillet in December, de Gaulle underwent a change of heart. He felt that Macmillan was hedging, that the Labor party was pressuring the Tories to make as few concessions as possible to gain admission to the EEC, and that the Tory party under Macmillan was hesitating to make Britain's entrance into the Common Market part of the election platform, since there was no doubt that public opinion in Britain was against membership.

During the Rambouillet meeting, de Gaulle said that he wanted Britain to join the Common Market but that he did not wish to change the character of Europe. He felt that Britain looked at the EEC as a free trade zone rather than as a group of countries with common economic rules. If the United Kingdom were permitted to join the EEC without acceptance of common rules, she and her Commonwealth "would dissolve Europe in the Atlantic Sea."[11]

In the long run, British membership was desirable, since France could not contain West Germany by herself. In principle, therefore, de Gaulle accepted British participation in Europe, but at this point in time British participation was not acceptable.

At the Rambouillet meeting, the joint effort to build the supersonic transport Concorde was discussed, but de Gaulle also brought up the subject of the defunct British ballistic missile Blue Streak. He proposed that Britain revive Blue Streak in collaboration with France instead of making new arrangements with the United States. Macmillan's failure to reply gave de Gaulle cause to claim that Macmillan was not interested in a European policy; yet only months before, at the Château de Champs, he had proposed joint defense cooperation with France after Britain's entrance into the Common Market.

No sooner had Macmillan met with de Gaulle at Rambouillet than he was off to Nassau for a meeting with President Kennedy. The two men spoke in detail about the multilateral nuclear force (MLF) that had been worked out during the last years of the Eisenhower administration by the various U.S. governmental agencies. The MLF was to be a mixed manned fleet of surface ships or submarines armed with Polaris missiles, jointly owned and operated by various NATO members, each of which would have a veto over the use of nuclear weapons.[12] The plan received only lukewarm endorsement from President Kennedy, who was unwilling to force this plan on the Europeans. Kennedy would agree to the MLF for Europe only under two conditions: the Europeans must pay their fair share of the expenditures, and the United States must retain a veto over the use of these weapons.

At the Nassau Conference, Kennedy offered Macmillan Polaris missiles provided that Britain would assign her Polaris fleet to NATO with the right to take it back whenever supreme national interests required. The offer was accepted by Macmillan.

Kennedy was ready to make the same offer to de Gaulle provided that France also put her nuclear submarines under NATO with the same right to take the fleet back whenever her supreme national interests were at stake. Kennedy and Macmillan discussed the offer they would make to de Gaulle in detail. They knew that the chances of de Gaulle's acceptance were fifty-fifty at best but hoped, nevertheless, that he would appreciate the offer enough to permit the passage of Britain's bid for membership in the Common Market. This offer represented an attempt by Kennedy to show de Gaulle that the United States was putting Franco-American relations on the same plane with Anglo-American relations.

Here, some Gaullist writers point out that Kennedy's offer to de Gaulle was not genuine, since he knew that France did not have the submarines from which these missiles could be launched nor the thermonuclear warheads to arm them, and therefore could not accept this offer.

However, these writers may not be aware of the fact that two weeks after Kennedy's meeting with Macmillan, the United States and Great Britain were willing to go one step further in an attempt to woo de Gaulle into partnership with them. On January 3, 1963, the American ambassador to France, Charles Bohlen, had a lengthy meeting with de Gaulle, and two days later British Ambassador Dixon did likewise. Both ambassadors led de Gaulle to understand that if he accepted their offer of Polaris missiles, anything France required in addition to Polaris would be made available. Besides submarine technology, thermonuclear warheads or the necessary design information or both would be provided. Dixon almost begged de Gaulle to accept and even attempted to revive de Gaulle's idea of a tridirectorate in NATO to coordinate global strategy.[13]

Militarily, this would have meant a modern nuclear force for France, putting her possibly a decade ahead of where she would be if she attempted to build such a fleet for herself. Besides, if she attempted to build such a fleet for herself, she might run the risk that her nuclear weapons would be obsolete before they became operational. Accepting the American offer would not only mean an enormous financial savings for France but at the same time make her the third nuclear power of the West, giving her parity with Great Britain and permanent superiority over West Germany.

But de Gaulle was not tempted by this offer even for a moment. If Kennedy and Macmillan had understood de Gaulle's "Grand Design," they would never have bothered to make such an offer, even though it was genuine and no one can deny that it was an exceptionally good one. De Gaulle wanted French supremacy in Western Europe. By accepting this offer, he would have been obliged to admit Britain into the EEC at that time, and

France would no longer have been the sole nuclear power in the Market. Furthermore, this offer showed no understanding of de Gaulle's dedication to a Europe free of American influence and only served to make de Gaulle's veto of Britain, which he called an American satellite, easier.[14] At the very moment the offer was made, de Gaulle was making preparations for a Western Europe led by France, and the first step in his plan was the Franco-German Treaty of Cooperation.

De Gaulle Says No to Britain

All Europe was stunned by de Gaulle's veto of British admission into the Common Market when it came in January, 1963. In his press conference of January 14, 1963, he gave a detailed account of his feelings about British membership in the Common Market:

The Treaty of Rome was concluded between six continental States, States which are, in short, economically of the same nature. . . . There are more similarities than differences between them.

It must be added, moreover, that from the standpoint of their economic development, their social progress and their technological capability, they are, in short, in stride with each other and they are moving forward at more or less the same pace. Furthermore, it happens that there exists between them no kind of political grievance, no border disputes, no rivalry for domination or power. To the contrary, there is a feeling of solidarity between them, firstly owing to the awareness they have of together possessing an important part of the origins of our civilization, and also with regard to their security, because they are continental countries. . . . Finally, they have a feeling of solidarity because not one of them is linked on the outside by any special political or military agreement.

. . . England is, in effect, insular, maritime, linked through its trade, markets and food supply to very diverse and often distant countries. Its activities are essentially industrial and commercial, and only slightly agricultural. It has, throughout its work, very marked and original customs and traditions. In short, the nature, structure and economic context of England differ profoundly from those of the States of the Continent.

. . . For example, the means by which the peoples of Great Britain nourish themselves is in fact by importing foodstuffs purchased at low prices in the two Americas or in the former dominions, while still granting large subsidies to British farmers. This means is obviously incompatible with the system the Six have quite naturally set up for themselves.

The system of the Six consists of making a pool of the agricultural products of the entire Community, of strictly determining their prices, of forbidding subsidizing, of organizing their consumption between all of the members and of making it obligatory for each of these members to pay to the Community any savings they might make by having foodstuffs brought in from outside instead of consuming those offered by the Common Market.

. . . The question is to know if Great Britain can at present place itself, with the Continent and like it, within a tariff that is truly common, give up all preferences with regard to the Commonwealth, cease to claim that its agriculture be privileged and, even more, consider as null and void the commitments it has made with the countries that are part of its free trade area. That question is the one at issue.[15]

De Gaulle said that if Britain would transform herself enough to belong to the European Economic Community without restriction or reservation and place the Common Market above anything else, France would no longer object to British membership.

According to one of de Gaulle's biographers, the General is supposed to have said in private about France's veto of Britain's membership in the EEC that the other five members of the Common Market would scream and kick and then would get used to it. Then he made another of his so accurate predictions. He contended that after a disastrous Labor government, a new Tory government under Edward Heath would enter the Common Market.[16]

But de Gaulle's decision to veto British entry did have serious repercussions. Although the other five finally accepted France's proposal for the financing of agriculture within the Common Market, they rejected de Gaulle's plan for political unity (Fouchet plan).

Actually the Fouchet plan was presented to the other five members of the Common Market in early 1962. The plan espoused a very loose confederation of the European Six, a union of sovereign states. De Gaulle believed that any separation between politics and economics is arbitrary and that one cannot take any important economic measure without committing a political act. He suggested that the Six form a political commission, a commission of defense, and a cultural commission just as they had already formed an economic commission.

Since there already existed within the EEC, EURATOM, and the European Coal and Steel Community common policies among the Six in the realms of economics, atomic energy, and coal and steel, Christian Fouchet, the French ambassador to the EEC, suggested that the essential end of his plan for political cooperation was a common foreign and defense policy for the European Six.

The other members of the Common Market were more favorably inclined toward a supranational Europe with British membership in this Europe, while de Gaulle thought more in terms of a political Europe of the Six, a loose confederation with each retaining full sovereignty. Of the five other members, Germany, who also favored a supranational Europe, was the most inclined to compromise and accept the Fouchet plan, while the Netherlands remained most insistent on a supranational Europe with British participation. De Gaulle said in numerous speeches that Great Britain would be even less inclined than France to be part of a supranational Europe. It appeared that he was technically correct, and by the spring of 1962 the other five were at the point where they would agree to compromise and accept de Gaulle's version of Europe provided that he would admit Great Britain. But just about this time, de Gaulle's feelings about British membership in the Common Market became more negative. After de Gaulle's veto of British membership, most of the other members of the EEC felt that with Britain out of Europe they would now settle for nothing less than a supranational Europe. The Fouchet plan came to nothing. The Benelux countries were the most opposed.

Franco-German Treaty
of Cooperation, 1963

Following this rebuff, de Gaulle turned to Germany, and in September, 1962, during President Lubke's visit to France, it was decided to begin between the two that which had not been possible to achieve among the Six. Both men agreed that the aim of Franco-German cooperation was the evolution toward a real political union of Western Europe. Political cooperation was to start first between France and West Germany in the hope that it would serve as the cornerstone around which the other four members of the Common Market would soon rally.

The Franco-German Treaty of Cooperation was signed on January 22, 1963. However, this treaty, which provided for cooperation between the two countries in the fields of foreign policy, defense, and education, proved to be somewhat less than de Gaulle, Adenauer, and the German Gaullists had hoped.[17] Although de Gaulle hailed this treaty in a speech he delivered in Bonn on July 3, 1964, he also added: "Let us not expect it to produce wonders every day."

The failure of the treaty to produce the benefits originally anticipated resulted from differences in French and German foreign policy on a variety of issues. In his press conference of July 23, 1964, de Gaulle openly admitted that Franco-German cooperation had not led to harmony between the policies of the two countries in Eastern Europe in general and on the question of the frontiers of Germany in particular. West Germany did not recognize the transfer of forty thousand square miles of former German land east of the Oder and Neisse rivers to Poland after World War II, while France did. Whereas France maintained diplomatic relations with all nations of Eastern Europe except the German Democratic Republic, West Germany maintained diplomatic relations with no Communist country except the USSR at that time. West Germany clung to the Hallstein doctrine of breaking diplomatic relations with any country that recognized the Pankow (East German) regime. It is one of the ironies of history that the German Federal Republic exempted only the USSR from this requirement. De Gaulle was not at all in agreement with the Hallstein doctrine, and his attitude toward Eastern Europe was one of accommodation and cooperation in the political, social, cultural, economic, and educational fields.

France also maintained a reserved attitude toward the creation of a multilateral nuclear force in NATO, which West Germany favored. In the military domain the German Federal Republic believed in a common defense within the framework of the Atlantic Alliance and the integration of the allied armed forces. De Gaulle believed that the armed forces of each country should be under the control of the government having jurisdiction over the country.

In the economic domain, the German Federal Republic wanted the Common Market to serve as the springboard for the unification of Western Europe, with the admission of Great Britain and other candidate states and a lowering of customs tariffs through negotiations. De Gaulle opposed British entry into the EEC under the present circumstances and did not favor the unification of Europe. Instead, he proposed a political unity of the Six, a so-called Europe of nations, not a supranational state, and did not support a lowering of customs tariffs.

Coalition, Not Integration

During the remaining years of de Gaulle's presidency, his attitude toward NATO, the testing of nuclear weapons, and the Common Market would result in strained relations between France and her Western allies. It was his adverse attitude toward integration that accounted for France's withdrawal from NATO, refusal to sign the Nuclear Test Ban Treaty of 1963, and continuous opposition to a supranational Western Europe. In each of these cases, his opposition to integration was based on his conclusion that political conditions had vastly changed since 1945 and that Europe should adapt itself to these changes.

At his press conference of May 15, 1962, de Gaulle said that the Atlantic Alliance would remain necessary so long as the USSR continued to threaten the world. He felt that within the Atlantic Alliance, however, the military organization known as NATO was functioning exactly as it had when the alliance was signed even though conditions in Europe had vastly changed. When the alliance was founded, only the United States and perhaps Great Britain possessed nuclear weapons. Western Europe found it expedient to turn over to the United States the responsibility for its own protection. De Gaulle continued to point out at this press conference that throughout this entire period the major portion of American and British land, air, and naval forces were not integrated into NATO, while all armaments France possessed in Europe belonged to NATO. French forces overseas were, however, not part of NATO.

By this time France's former colonies in Black Africa had become independent, and de Gaulle knew that Algeria would be an independent country within weeks. Most of the French forces overseas had already returned to metropolitan France, and the remainder were to return from Algeria as soon as independence took effect. Therefore, de Gaulle wanted to assure that French forces returning from overseas would not be integrated into NATO. He felt that it was necessary for France to make her army a more integral part of the nation, to restation it on French soil, and to make her defense once again a national defense.

France did not take part in the Geneva Conference on Disarmament, which got under way in 1962. De Gaulle believed that nothing would come out of this conference, since neither the United States nor the USSR would agree to do away with their arms. On numerous occasions he had proposed the banning of vehicles for delivery of nuclear warheads such as rockets, airplanes, and submarines; and since he did not believe there was any chance of such a measure being adopted at Geneva, there was no point in French participation. De Gaulle insisted that France would welcome total disarmament with open arms but so long as there was no disarmament, France would have to continue to arm herself. He said that disarmament was not the aim of the United States, the USSR, and Great Britain. Their aim was not to disarm those who were armed but to prevent those who were not armed from arming. France refused to sign the Nuclear Test Ban Treaty in July, 1963, because de Gaulle felt that his country must carry out nuclear tests and gather necessary data if she was to have an independent policy of her own.[18] He also questioned whether the United States would use her nuclear weapons to defend Europe, and, if so, how these weapons would be used. For this reason, he felt that France must have her own.

At the same time, President Kennedy came out against the dispersion of nuclear weapons to national governments and in favor of a multilateral nuclear force (MLF) in NATO under United States control. The United States might well have feared that if her allies acquired nuclear weapons, she could more easily be dragged into a war against her own will.

De Gaulle seemed to be on the way to a head-on collision with Kennedy, since he was becoming more insistent that all armies, military equipment, supplies, and stockpiles within a country be under strict supervision of the government of that country. It was his sincere conviction that France must have her own national defense. Allies were always essential, according to de Gaulle's way of thinking, but alliances had no absolute virtues apart from the sentiments on which they were based; and, if one were to lose the free disposition of oneself, there was a strong risk of never regaining it. The very fact that France was now in danger of being destroyed was enough to justify both alliance with the United States and independence from her as well.

De Gaulle felt that so long as the United States was the only country in the world to possess nuclear weapons, France was free from danger, since no nation would dare to attack an ally of the United States. He said that it was sensible when the Atlantic Alliance was organized for the tactical and strategic air force to be under American command, since airplanes were at the time the only means of delivering atomic weapons. Since the time of organization, however, not only had the USSR acquired nuclear weapons, but new and better missiles made it possible for the United States and the USSR to launch an attack directly from each other's soil. Under these circumstances, de Gaulle said, it was not possible to tell how American nuclear weapons would be employed to defend Europe. Even though he agreed that American nuclear weapons remained the essential guarantee of world peace, he believed that American nuclear power did not meet all the eventualities concerning France and Europe. Thus it was necessary for France to equip herself with a nuclear force of her own.

With regard to the proposal by the United States to give France Polaris missiles provided that she put her entire fleet under NATO, de Gaulle affirmed that it would be contrary to France's principle of defense to turn French weapons over to a multilateral force under foreign command, for there would be no guarantee as to the use of these weapons.

During de Gaulle's press conference of July 29, 1963, he criticized as excessive the outbursts against him in the American press and restated the fundamental factors of Franco-American relations, friendship, and alliance. He delved into the historic ties between France and the United States, recalling how they had fought side by side in three wars, and contended that only a long period of dissension between the two countries could sever Franco-American relations. After admitting that there were political divergences between Paris and Washington, he reaffirmed the basic necessity of the Atlantic Alliance and said that France would again be at the side of the United States in the event of a war. For France, friendship with the United States was the first order of business.

In de Gaulle's mind the divergences between the two countries over the Atlantic Alliance were purely and simply the result of intrinsic changes that had taken place in the previous few years with regard to their relative power. France had simply become stronger than she had previously been.

In his press conference of January 31, 1964, de Gaulle came

down hard against certain Common Market countries (which he did not mention by name) that were blocking his plan for a political union of the Six by formulating three unattainable and contradictory goals: (1) no European Union without integration under supranational leadership; (2) no European Union without the incorporation of Great Britain; (3) no European Union not incorporated into the Atlantic Community.[19] With regard to the first point, de Gaulle said that the peoples of Europe would never submit to the authority of an assembly composed mainly of foreigners. With regard to the second, he said that England would be the last nation in Europe to accept this kind of integration; and third, to merge the policy of Europe into a multilateral Atlantic policy would be tantamount to Europe's having no policy itself, and in that case there would be no need for such a union.

De Gaulle was convinced that a European union (supranational Europe) incorporated into the Atlantic Community would be an Atlantic Europe without a personality or policy and therefore politically subordinate to the United States.[20] On the other hand, a political union of European nations, a Europe of the Six, would retain its own personality. It would be a European (not an Atlantic) Europe, existing by itself and for itself, and would have a policy of its own. A European Europe meant an independent Europe, a restored Europe, that historic center of economic activity, civilization, and power capable once again of having its influence felt in the world. A contribution toward a European settlement, that is to say, agreement between Eastern and Western Europe, would be made by the economic and political union of Western Europe. De Gaulle believed that the future of Europe depended upon the normalization of relations among all European countries.[21]

De Gaulle repeated that only the governments of nations were capable of and responsible for making policy. The day might well come when all the peoples of Europe would become one, and then there could be a Government of Europe; but it would be ridiculous according to him to act as if that day had arrived.

At his press conference of July 23, 1964, de Gaulle spoke of the division of the world into two camps as a result of World War II. Fortunately, he added, that division corresponded less and less to the real situation. The monolithic nature of the totalitarian world was in the process of dislocation, and the USSR was seeing China contest the domination she exercised over vast regions of Asia and the European satellites she had subjugated by force moving farther and farther away. Compared to the systems of Western Europe, communism had already met with failure with respect to the standard of living and the satisfaction, dignity, and freedom of men.

Under these changed circumstances, de Gaulle could see that Western Europe was being called upon to play a role of its own. It should maintain an alliance with the United States so long as the Soviet threat remained, but the reasons that originally made this alliance subordinate to the United States were rapidly fading. A strong and independent Western Europe politically and economically united, which would assume its own responsibilities and side with the United States, should be in the interest of the United States.

Premier Georges Pompidou stated before the National Assembly that de Gaulle and the French government would not only continue to oppose the idea of European integration (a supranational Europe), but at the same time would promote the idea of the political union of the European Six. He posed the question of why the nations that assert the necessity of integration are the same ones that insist that Great Britain, which would be the last nation to accept integration, must belong to this community. Pompidou concluded that the only possible answer was that these nations wanted to build an "Atlantic" Europe, a Europe that would give up its political personality, its European defense and European foreign policy, limiting itself to organizing its economic and social life through a supranational framework while leaving its defense and foreign policy as well as political personality to be defined by the United States.

Pompidou also spoke about France's testing of nuclear weapons and the fact that France had the right to disagree with the United States on her intervention in Vietnam and the Dominican Republic just as the United States had disagreed with French policy in the Middle East in 1956. But he was emphatic in assuring that France was turning her back neither on the United States, whom she regarded as her friend and ally, nor on the Atlantic Alliance, which still remained a necessity.[22]

France Quits NATO

De Gaulle's twelfth press conference, on September 9, 1965,

proved to be a memorable one. After reaffirming his commitment to the Atlantic Alliance, he said that France's adherence to this alliance was conditional upon her being able to pursue an independent course of action. Therefore, he served notice that upon the expiration of the North Atlantic Treaty in 1969, France would no longer participate in NATO, the military organization that provided for the integration of the armed forces of the member states, but would remain loyal to the alliance itself.[23]

At his press conference of February 21, 1966, de Gaulle spoke about the Atlantic Alliance and NATO. He stated:

Nothing can make a law enforceable, without amendment, when it no longer agrees with the ways of the times. Nothing can make a treaty wholly valid when its object has changed. Nothing can make an alliance remain as such when the conditions in which it was concluded have changed. It is therefore necessary to adapt the law, the treaty and the alliance to the new factors, failing which, the texts, emptied of their substance, will, if circumstances so require, be nothing more than useless papers in the archives, unless there is a harsh break between these obsolete forms and the living realities.[24]

De Gaulle felt that the Atlantic Alliance remained valid for France but recognized that the measures for implementation taken subsequently no longer corresponded to what France deemed satisfactory with respect to herself. His reasoning in the matter was pure and simple. When NATO was formed, only the United States possessed nuclear weapons. When the USSR first possessed them, she was still not able to strike directly at the United States, but the United States could hit the USSR from Europe. Now that both superpowers were capable of destroying each other from their own soil, Europe had become a second line of defense for the United States. France was already modifying the measures currently practiced with regard to integration in preparation for the withdrawal of all of her forces from the integrated NATO command.

In another speech before the National Assembly on April 20, 1966, Premier Georges Pompidou announced that France had decided to begin her withdrawal from NATO and that the process was to be completed before the expiration of the Atlantic Alliance. He explained that de Gaulle had chosen now as the time to withdraw because he hoped that all would be settled between France and her allies when the alliance came up for renewal in

1969. Soon, de Gaulle would reduce the time allocated for French withdrawal from NATO to two years before the time for renewal (April, 1967).

Pompidou affirmed France's need to withdraw from NATO starting immediately and to resume full exercise of her sovereignty on her soil and in her skies but said that she would remain faithful to the Atlantic Alliance. France's partners, according to Pompidou, did not seem ready to reform the organization but only seemed determined to maintain the existing organization.

Integration, according to de Gaulle, was a product of the Cold War and could involve France in a conflict against her will. He wanted a freely agreed upon alliance, an alliance among equals. Before any nation could be an independent and equal ally, he added, it was essential that it have at its disposal a military force of some standing.

One of de Gaulle's major arguments in opposing integration was that it created risks for France. He cited the Cuban missile crisis as an example. Before the French government was even consulted about the crisis, and while NATO forces were supposed to be outside the conflict, American forces in Europe including those in France were placed in a state of alert. If the United States and the USSR had become involved in a war over Cuba, who could say that the fact of having on French soil the American General Headquarters in Europe with its communications network and its entire command apparatus as well as air bases and supply depots would not constitute an obvious and serious risk for France and make her a target for atomic bombs?

By September, 1966, steps at evacuating American bases, as well as all organs of NATO, from French soil were well under way. Starting July 1, 1966, all the NATO commands in France began to withdraw and were being reinstalled outside France. The entire process had to be completed by April 1, 1967.

Treaty of Rome

It seemed that de Gaulle was also opposed to a proposal in the Treaty of Rome which stipulated that in 1966 the Council of Ministers, the so-called policy-making body of the Common Market, would be authorized to make decisions on the basis of a majority rather than a unanimous vote. This plan seemed incompatible with de Gaulle's idea of the sovereignty of nations. He pointed out that in the past workings of the Common Market, one or two of its members had been able to prevent the organization from moving on to a more advanced stage of development when it had not yet solved old problems. If the member nations had been permitted to proceed over the objections of one or two of its members, there never would have been, for instance, a Common Market agricultural policy. Only because unanimity had been the rule before 1966 had France succeeded in convincing other Common Market nations that agriculture should be included in the economic sector.

A compromise was finally reached which stipulated that the council's decisions on coal and steel would be taken by a majority vote; on fundamental matters of policy concerning the Common Market, a unanimous vote was still required; while on other (nonfundamental) matters, a two-thirds majority vote was sufficient. [25]

At his press conference of October 28, 1966, de Gaulle said that in this changing world nothing had remained more constant than France's policy. This policy, he emphasized, was that France must be, and must remain, an independent nation so that she can play her own role in the world. He continued:

It is true that, among our contemporaries, there are many minds—and often some of the best—who have envisaged that our country renounce its independence under the cover of one or another international grouping. Having thus handed over to foreign bodies the responsibility for our destiny, our leaders would—according to the expression sanctioned by that school of thought—have nothing more to do than "plead France's case."

. . . Thus some—exalting in the dream of the international—wanted to see our country place itself, as they placed themselves, under the obedience of Moscow. Thus others—invoking either the supranational myth, or the danger from the East, or the advantage that the Atlantic West could derive from unifying its economy, or even the imposing utility of world arbitration—maintained that France should allow her policy to be dissolved in a tailor-made Europe, her defense in NATO, her monetary concepts in the Washington Fund, her personality in the United Nations, et cetera.

Certainly, it is a good thing that such institutions exist, and it is only in our interest to belong to them; but if we had listened to their extreme apostles, these organs in which, as everyone knows, the political protection, military protection, economic power and multiform aid of the United States predominate—these organs would have been for us only a cover for our submission to American hegemony. Thus, France would disappear swept away by illusions.[26]

During this same press conference, he spoke of the Common Market and said it must continue its development in order to define a policy that was European, a statement he had made time and time again. This time, however, he added that even if the economic Six accepted the French plan for political union, nothing valid or sound could be done in Europe so long as the peoples of the East and the West had not reached an agreement. By 1966, de Gaulle had undertaken what he considered the most important step in his foreign policy, a détente with the Communist East. He was actually saying that his plan for the economic and political union of Western Europe, a loose confederation of the Six, should be only the first step in his "Grand Design" of establishing one Europe, a loose confederation of sovereign states from the Atlantic to the Urals.

De Gaulle also spoke of France's regaining her independence in the international domain and the fact that she had not been spending more on defense since the time she had decided to withdraw from NATO. He spoke against the continuance of a double hegemony in which the two superpowers would possess the means for ensuring their own security through deterrence and would hold under their obedience their own camp of committed peoples. The situation could in the long run only serve to paralyze and sterilize the rest of the world by placing it under this double hegemony, he said. He ended by saying that France became an atomic power at the time that her independence in matters of defense was restored, but added that France did not wish to extend herself beyond her own soil either ideologically, politically, or economically and would not become involved in a conflict against her will.

The subject of British entry into the Common Market again presented itself in 1967, the tenth anniversary of the signing of the Treaty of Rome. De Gaulle agreed to journey to Rome for a summit conference with the leaders of the Common Market countries. He did not change his opinion about membership, but the tone of his speeches on this subject showed a slight softening in his attitude over the years.

At his press conference of May 16, 1967, he said that Great Britain was not a continental power but rather an island, and, because of the Commonwealth, committed beyond the seas. In addition, she was tied to the United States by all sorts of agreements. For these reasons she did not merge into the EEC when it was taking shape.

The main problem with regard to Britain's entry into the Common Market was in the field of agriculture. Britain imported cheap food from the Commonwealth nations and, if she were to subscribe to the Common Market, she would have to levy import duties on these foodstuffs and raise the price of her food. If she were allowed to enter without being subjected to the agricultural system of the Six, the system would collapse, according to de Gaulle, completely upsetting the equilibrium of the Common Market.

Another problem, according to de Gaulle, was that while the currencies of the Common Market countries circulated freely, British capital was not permitted to leave the country in order that her balance of trade deficit could be limited. If Britain permitted the pound to leave the country freely, that currency would be further weakened. The Common Market currencies were sound, and if one of the currencies were threatened, the other five could ensure its recovery at little cost to themselves. De Gaulle insisted that monetary parity and solidarity were essential conditions for admission into the Market and could not be extended to Britain until her currency showed more strength and stability.

De Gaulle said that the Common Market nations had to make one of three choices with regard to Great Britain:

1. Admit her under present conditions. This would necessitate building up an entirely new edifice, scrapping all that had been built so far.
2. Establish between the Common Market and Great Britain and other members of the "free trade area" a system of association that would leave the Common Market unchanged yet be of benefit to both groups.
3. Wait for Great Britain to make the appropriate changes from within, since she was already showing signs of making the necessary economic and political transformations to enable her to qualify for membership in the EEC.[27]

Nothing in these statements, however, indicated that France would block British membership.

In an interview granted by Foreign Minister Couve de Murville to the French weekly *l'Express* on June 5, 1967, he said that the summit talks in Rome had been useful and that the Council of Ministers of the EEC in Brussels was studying the request for British entry into the organization. He also mentioned that West Germany and Italy had been showing interest in political cooperation while the Benelux countries objected to starting along the road to political cooperation without British participation.

Kurt Kiesinger, who became chancellor of the German Federal Republic in 1966, seemed to be taking a more pro-Gaullist position than his predecessor Ludwig Erhard, but markedly less pro-Gaullist than that of Adenauer. Nevertheless, the Franco-German Treaty of Cooperation was again showing signs of rebirth under Kiesinger.

De Gaulle spoke at length about Great Britain's new bid to enter the Common Market in his press conference of November 27, 1967, likening this bid to the fifth act of a play:

Actually, we are viewing here the fifth act of a play during which Britain's very diverse behaviors with regard to the Common Market have succeeded one another without seeming to be alike.

The first act had been London's refusal to participate in the drafting of the Rome Treaty, which it was thought across the Channel would never come to anything. The second act brought out Britain's deep-seated hostility toward European construction, once that construction started to take shape. . . . The third act was the negotiations conducted in Brussels by Mr. Maudling for a year and a half, negotiations designed to make the Community bow to Britain's conditions and halted when France made her partners note that the issue involved was not whether the Community should bow to Britain's conditions, but precisely the opposite. The fourth act, at the start of Mr. Wilson's Government, was marked by London's lack of interest in the Common Market, the maintenance around Great Britain of the six other European States forming the free-trade area, and a great effort exerted to strengthen the Commonwealth's internal ties. And now the fifth act is being played for which Great Britain, this time, has declared her candidacy, and, in order for it to be adopted, has set out on the path of all the promises and all the pressures imaginable.[28]

De Gaulle felt that Britain was again turning to the continent because of the enormous power of the United States, the growing power of the USSR, the rebirth of power of the continental states, the new power of China, and the new centrifugal orientations of the Commonwealth. He said that Britain's entrance into Europe would be beneficial to her and satisfactory to Europe, but she must first make the necessary internal and external adjustments. If Britain were to enter the Common Market without making such adjustments, it would mean the breaking up of the community that had been built according to rules that did not tolerate such monumental exceptions.

De Gaulle said that he desired to see Britain in the Common Market one day soon and that he recognized the psychological evolution taking shape in Great Britain. He congratulated the British on certain steps they had already taken and others they planned to take toward establishing their balance from within and their external independence from foreign powers.[29] He felt that future negotiations on this subject would depend on whether or not the British people wanted to make their country one of the pillars of a European Europe.

The Monetary Problem

The international monetary crisis that had flared up from time to time since 1965 had become acute by November, 1967. At an earlier press conference of February 4, 1965, de Gaulle gave his view of the international monetary situation. His opinion, like all others, was based on the premise that the international situation had changed since 1945. At that time war and inflation were ruining all European currencies, and nearly all of the world's gold reserves were held by the United States. At Bretton Woods, an agreement was signed which set up a "gold exchange standard." Dollars and gold became almost indistinguishable. The dollar was pegged to gold and all other currencies to the dollar. The United States was at an advantage in international trade, since gold became the medium for settling foreign balances of payments throughout the world, and she experienced no difficulty in settling her debts in gold if asked to do so.

De Gaulle emphasized that the conditions that had given rise to the gold exchange standard had changed. The Bretton Woods agreement was out of date, since the Common Market nations combined already held greater gold reserves than the United States. It was unfair to allow the United States to settle her deficits in the balance of payments by simply exporting dollars, because dollars were no longer as good as gold. He said in the February 4, 1965, press conference that "circumstances are such today that it is possible to wonder how far difficulties would go if the states which hold dollars sooner or later reached the point where they wanted to convert them into gold."[30]

De Gaulle did not have to say more. It does not take an economist to figure out that the mass selling of dollars by states holding them in return for gold would ultimately result in the devaluation of the dollar.

When he began to unload his dollars for gold, thereby helping to precipitate an international monetary crisis in 1967, it is questionable whether he was hoping for a devaluation of the dollar. First among all of his considerations, he preferred to hold gold to dollars at that point in case of a dollar devaluation. Second, and probably nearly as important, he wanted to show the world that if other nations followed France's lead and sold their dollars for gold, the international monetary system would collapse. Therefore, the system had to be revised as soon as possible. De Gaulle's solution to the problem was to peg all foreign currencies to gold, since no currency had any value except by direct or indirect relation to gold real or supposed. If his solution were to find acceptance among the Western leaders, France would be in an advantageous position, since she had already sold many of her dollars for gold. Unfortunately for de Gaulle, none of the other leaders of industrial nations favored his solution to the monetary problem.

By 1968, the Common Market nations had reached an agreement on an external tariff, and a common agricultural policy that de Gaulle had urged for such a long time found acceptance as well. But he continued to warn that the Common Market should be enlarged only with extreme caution. The Six had not agreed to undertake political unity among themselves, and de Gaulle asked how much more difficult this task would be if the Market were enlarged to include ten, twelve, or fourteen members.

During his press conference of September 9, 1968, de Gaulle spoke mainly about subjects he had touched on in the past but added that France had been working to end the system of the two power blocs and had detached herself from the military organization of NATO, which subordinated Europeans to Americans. De Gaulle was saying yes to alliances between independent nations freely entered into and no to subordination of Europeans by Americans and Russians in two power blocs and the division of Europe into American and Soviet spheres of influence.

De Gaulle should have been riding high in the fall of 1968.

The riots and demonstrations in the spring of that year had led him to dissolve parliament and call for new elections. The obvious backlash in provincial France against Communist and other left-wing demonstrators in the spring accounted for a landslide victory for the Gaullist deputies in the June parliamentary elections.[31] But in spite of the massive landslide the Gaullists had received, the new warmth that characterized France's relations with the USSR and Eastern Europe, the place of honor reserved for France in the eyes of the developing nations, all was not going well for de Gaulle. The franc had become weak, de Gaulle's ability to speak for Western Europe had declined, and he had to cut back on his strategic weapons program due to the critical economic situation.

The financial situation was his biggest problem. Large amounts of money had left France after the crisis of the spring and continued to do so as the months passed. The government tried to reinvigorate the economy by a program of expansion. Too much credit was made available and the government found itself contributing to the flow of hot money.[32] By November 15, the Western world was gripped by a new financial crisis, and this time the pressure was on the franc. Devaluation, it was believed, was inevitable. The question was how great a devaluation was needed. Estimates ranged from a conservative 8 percent to an astounding 25 percent.[33]

Some of the ten leading industrial countries in the International Monetary Fund believed that the best solution would be for West Germany to revalue and possibly spare de Gaulle the need to devalue. The United States and Great Britain backed France in an attempt to get the West German government to revalue the mark. If the franc fell under too great pressure, the dollar and the pound sterling would be next to suffer, because of their positions as reserve currencies. But West Germany said no to revaluation, and on November 20, Europe's major foreign exchange markets were closed.

Before de Gaulle's speech, broadcast live over French radio and television on Sunday, November 24, 1968, the United States and several others in the International Monetary Fund offered de Gaulle two billion dollars to support the franc (most of which was supplied by the United States), provided that his devaluation not exceed 10 percent. De Gaulle's acceptance enabled him to announce on November 24 his decision not to devalue at all, but he was only postponing the inevitable. In return for this pledge of assistance, de Gaulle had to promise not to sell any more dollars for gold.

The German attitude during this entire crisis bothered de Gaulle as well as other Western leaders. Germany had said no to de Gaulle before, but never since the end of World War II had she said no to the United States, Great Britain, and France at the same time. This new assertiveness on the part of the Germans made de Gaulle think seriously about improving relations with Great Britain and the United States during his last few months in office. He was seriously beginning to consider bringing Great Britain into the Common Market with a minimum of concessions on her part, in order to balance the growing economic power of West Germany. Since Britain, as he had always said, would be more opposed to the idea of a supranational Europe than France, this treatment might serve to rid the other five of these idealistic dreams and lead them to think in terms of de Gaulle's vision of a Europe of states, a loose confederation.

For a while he even toyed with the idea of replacing the Common Market with a free-trade area in which Great Britain, Ireland, Scandinavia, and Western Europe could participate. Political cooperation would revolve around Great Britain, France, West Germany, and Italy, the four largest countries. De Gaulle did continue to stress the importance of an independent Europe and noted that among the nations of Western Europe only France had achieved a large degree of independence from the United States.

In his last months in office, de Gaulle realized that if his vision of Europe were eventually to emerge, it would emerge slowly, not within his lifetime. What he did realize was that no European structure was possible without French presence, and that the Europe that ultimately emerged would be one in which France would play a major role.

CHAPTER 4

A New Dialogue with the USSR

PRESIDENT de Gaulle seemed ready to begin a new dialogue with the leaders of the USSR upon his return to power. It was a mere coincidence that 1958, the year de Gaulle returned to power, marked not only a political mutation for France but was the year in which relations between the USSR and the West were approaching the crossroads.

It should be recalled that the year 1956 marked the breach in the Eastern bloc. At the Twentieth Communist Party Congress in Moscow, Nikita Khrushchev said that each nation should develop its own road toward socialism within limits. The results of this speech were seen in the events that took place in Poland and Hungary in the fall of that year.

The year 1957 was marked not only by a summit conference among the leaders of the Warsaw Pact nations and a NATO conference, at which the Western allies examined ways in which they could deal collectively with the Eastern bloc, but by aggricultural improvements in the USSR and the launching of Sputnik. The prestige of the USSR began to soar.

In 1958, divergences between the USSR and Red China seemed to appear. The USSR was playing her diplomatic game in all fields. By the late winter and early spring of 1958, she put forth a series of proposals on peaceful coexistence, the forbidding of nuclear tests, and disarmament, but at the same time declared herself resolved to press forward by all means the "struggle of the people" against colonial powers.

With regard to nuclear tests the Soviet government claimed that the Cold War had made the solution of vital international problems highly complicated. It also argued that each government could contribute to halting the insane and wasteful armaments race and restoring common sense in international politics. The fact that eighty-two countries voted in favor of peaceful coexistence at the twelfth Session of the General Assembly of the United Nations shows that hundreds of millions throughout the world wished for a détente and a durable and lasting peace.[1]

In 1958 the Soviet government began to stress the Leninist principles of peaceful coexistence and competition between the social and economic systems of capitalism and socialism, asserting that peaceful coexistence was the cornerstone of Soviet socialist foreign policy. The USSR stated that the essential conditions for peaceful coexistence and competition of the two systems were the noninterference in one another's internal affairs, equality, mutual benefit, and respect for sovereignty and territorial integrity.

In this same year the USSR proposed various disarmament schemes. She unilaterally halted all atomic and nuclear tests above the surface and urged the United States and Great Britain to do likewise. The USSR refused to take any further part in the UN Disarmament Committee, claiming that the committee's main task was to deceive public opinion while preventing an agreement on disarmament. Instead, she and her allies submitted proposals for a complete and unconditional prohibition of nuclear weapons and for the creation of conditions in which atomic energy would be used solely for peaceful purposes. Yet the Soviet Union refused to accept a mutual system of aerial inspection proposed by the United States (Open Skies).

At the same time the USSR pressed forward the "struggle of the people" against colonial powers. The West was accused of neocolonial exploitation in the Middle East and in Latin America, while the European nations that still held colonies became victims of a verbal tirade. France was accused of abuses in Algeria, and Russia expressed her sympathy for the revolutionary Algerian movement.

Last, the USSR posed the problem of the status of Berlin in November, 1958. The USSR demanded that the three Western powers quit Berlin within six months and turn West Berlin into a free city. If the West refused to agree, the USSR would be forced to sign a separate peace treaty with East Germany, ending the status of the three Western powers in Berlin. On January 10, 1959, Russia called for a peace conference within the next two months to conclude a treaty with the two German states giving each state diplomatic recognition.

It appeared that the interests of France and the USSR could not have been farther apart at the end of 1958. De Gaulle was favorably disposed to a détente and did not wish to see the balance of power upset to France's disadvantage. Could the traditional friendship between France and Russia manifest itself again?

Three phases in Franco-Soviet relations can be distinguished during the period in which de Gaulle was president of the Fifth Republic: (1) from the time de Gaulle returned to power until the failure of the Paris Summit Conference of May, 1960, a tentative dialogue was drafted between Paris and Moscow about the difficulties of Algeria and the tension created around Berlin; (2) between May, 1960, and the end of 1963 friction between the two countries multiplied and Franco-Soviet relations deteriorated; (3) between January, 1964, and May, 1969, Franco-Soviet relations not only ameliorated but changed from poor to excellent.

When de Gaulle was about to become the last prime minister of the Fourth Republic of France and be given the power to draft a new constitution creating the Fifth Republic, the USSR labeled the possibility of de Gaulle's coming to power more bad than good. On the other hand, the Soviet Union looked upon this change as an opportunity to improve Franco-Soviet relations, which had more than once in history been amiable. So the initial Soviet attitude toward de Gaulle was one of watchful waiting.

De Gaulle Meets Adenauer

On September 14, 1958, three months after de Gaulle became prime minister of the Fourth Republic, but before he became president of the Fifth, Chancellor Konrad Adenauer journeyed to Colombey-les-Deux-Eglises for a meeting with de Gaulle at his home. A joint communiqué was issued in which the two men professed their attachment to close cooperation between France and West Germany as "the foundation for all constructive work in Europe." Actually, Adenauer had hesitated to journey to France and had feared the coming to power of de Gaulle because of his anti-German statements of the past. However, upon his meeting de Gaulle at his home in an atmosphere of hospitality and warmth, the two men took an immediate liking to each other. Adenauer returned to Germany optimistic about Franco-German friendship in the future.

The Soviet government reacted adversely to the Adenauer-de Gaulle meeting, accusing de Gaulle of trying to share with West Germany the leadership of a continental European bloc extending to the coast of Africa. De Gaulle was accused of taking a position at variance with his earlier remarks regarding Franco-Soviet cooperation, the European Defense Community, and German militarism.[2] Actually the Soviet Union feared that Franco-German cooperation might produce an integrated Western Europe in which West Germany, not France, would emerge as the senior partner because of her economic and military strength.

Khrushchev's Interview
with Pravda *on France*

On September 22, 1958, *Pravda* published an interview with Nikita Khrushchev dealing exclusively with the situation in France and the meeting between de Gaulle and Adenauer. Khrushchev said:

Three or four months ago, everyone in Europe was able to allow himself the hope that the new government having at its head General de Gaulle would have the will and power to subdue the fascist rebels, to put an end to an unjust colonial war against the people of Algeria, and to maintain the Republic in France. In truth, from the very beginning, progressive forces warned us that all of that was only vain and dangerous illusions, and that between the events of Algeria and the coming to power of the new government in Paris, there was the most direct and the most reciprocal tie.

The illusion about the mission of the new government became yet more apparent when this feverish race for the preparation of the new constitution, investing the chief of the government with the most far reaching dictatorial powers, began.[3]

Khrushchev went on to say that a fascist regime was about to inaugurate itself in France and that the new constitution was designed to establish a personal dictatorship. As for the rapprochement between the French and the Germans, Khrushchev recalled that, in the past, de Gaulle had spoken frequently about the German danger and reproached him for denying the existence of this danger at present.

Once the USSR posed the problem of the status of Berlin in November, 1958, relations between Russia and the West revolved around the Berlin crisis for the next several months. The French attitude toward the Soviet ultimatum on Berlin was even firmer than that of the United States and Great Britian, in that de

Gaulle had been pursuing a policy of good relations with Konrad Adenauer since their September meeting. De Gaulle said that the Soviet declaration ordering the three Western powers out of Berlin and the conversion of West Berlin into a free city should not lead the West away from the idea of the reunification of Germany on the basis of free elections. The agreements made by the Big Four over Germany and Berlin in 1945 were still legally binding and could not be put in question by Premier Khrushchev. De Gaulle assured the West Germans that Paris would not make any concessions to the USSR on the German problem, and even viewed Macmillan's trip to Moscow in February, 1959, as a concession to the Russians.

De Gaulle's Press Conference
of March 25, 1959

President de Gaulle would not budge one inch on the German problem and absolutely refused to recognize the East German regime as a sovereign and independent state, because it "could not have been born and could not exist except by virtue of the Soviet occupation and because of an implacable dictatorship."[4] De Gaulle went on to say that the French Republic could not put the German Democratic Republic on the same level as the German Federal Republic where citizens say, read and hear what they like, come and go as they please, and elect their representatives and their government with freedom of choice. The reunification of the two parts into a single Germany would seem to be the normal destiny of the German people within the present frontiers of the two German states.

It must be noted here that De Gaulle's stand on the unification of Germany within its present boundaries made him the first Western leader to acknowledge the permanent transfer to Poland of 40,000 square miles of German territory. This transfer had been made by the Potsdam Conference of 1945. The West claimed that the Potsdam Conference had only made a provisional transfer of this land to Poland and only a peace treaty with Germany putting a formal end to World War II could determine how much of this land Poland would be permitted to retain in the future. The USSR and her allies in Eastern Europe looked upon Poland's acquisition of this rich and valuable land as a permanent transfer.

De Gaulle would not agree to Soviet schemes of European disarmament by zones, which he claimed would be to the detriment of the West, unless the East withdrew as far as the Ural Mountains. However, de Gaulle spoke of the possibility of a meeting between the foreign ministers of the Big Four, which, if successful, could lead to a summit conference in the near future. He spoke of the traditional friendship between France and Russia.

This press conference came at a time when Soviet commentaries were unfavorable to the interior politics of France. Khrushchev, in a speech before the Twenty-first Communist Party Congress on January 27, 1959, had developed two themes and tried to connect the two. They were: the orientation of France toward a military dictatorship; the collusion between the governments of Paris and Bonn.

Tass on March 28, 1959, accused France of negating the German danger and reproached France for failing to recognize the German Democratic Republic. It was astonished at de Gaulle's proposal that a zone of limitation of armaments should extend to the Ural Mountains if the interests of the West were not to be harmed. Tass expressed its surprise at some of de Gaulle's statements since, in the past, de Gaulle had been among the first to recognize the German danger, especially in the 1930's. On the other hand, Tass commended de Gaulle for his recognition of the Oder and Neisse rivers as the permanent eastern boundary of Germany, which neither Great Britain nor the United States recognized as permanent at that time.

Soviet Attitude toward French Policies in Africa

African problems created several difficulties in the relations between France and the USSR in 1959. Moscow's attitude on Algeria was, however, discrete. It had not recognized the G.P.R.A. (Provisional Revolutionary Government of Algeria) established in 1958, but it nevertheless expressed sympathy for the Algerian people who were trying to throw off the colonial yoke. The Soviet government felt that the United Nations could play a role and exercise its influence so that Algeria could gain her independence. Moscow said that if France were to find a common language with the Algerians, it would be in her own interests. The Soviet attitude toward France's policies in Black Africa was a little harsher. The USSR regarded the creation of the French Community in Black Africa as a new form of colonial domination.

After Guinea's rupture with France in the referendum in 1958 and her rejection of the French Community, the USSR, Poland, Czechoslovakia, and the German Democratic Republic signed a-greements providing economic aid for the Guinean government in February, 1959. These agreements were followed in August by a Soviet loan of 140 million rubles and an additional agreement providing for economic and technical cooperation.

Geneva Conference of Foreign Ministers, May-August, 1959

The Soviet government had hoped for a summit conference in 1959, but the three Western powers favored a foreign ministers conference first. The Western position was accepted with the un-derstanding that if agreement could be reached on a few basic is-sues, a summit conference would follow soon after. At this con-ference, the two German states were represented by several counsellors.

Foreign Minister Andrei Gromyko of the USSR stressed the importance of signing a peace treaty with the two German states and refused to guarantee the present situation of the allies in West Berlin except for an intermediary period of one year and a half. This represented a softening of the original period of six months. France, along with Great Britain and the United States, defended the "peace plan" that was signed between the USSR and the three Western powers over Berlin in 1945 and held to the position that the interests of European security could best be served by the reunification of Germany step by step through free elections.

Although the positions of the USSR and the West were miles apart on Germany, Berlin, and disarmament, the atmosphere at these talks was not only cordial but friendly. As a result, Nikita Khrushchev was invited to visit the United States in September of that year.

After the Geneva Conference of Foreign Ministers, France felt that a détente was ensuing and that the time might be ripe for a summit conference in the spring of 1960. De Gaulle felt that the summit meeting should be preceded by a meeting between himself and Khrushchev, since Khrushchev had already met

Macmillan in Moscow in February, 1959, and Eisenhower in the United States in September, 1959. An invitation was extended to Premier Khrushchev to visit France, and on October 31, 1959, he announced his intention to visit France the following March.

De Gaulle felt that East-West relations had ameliorated over the past few months and that Moscow was acting with reserve by refraining from throwing fuel on the fire in the Third World. The exchange of notes between Khrushchev and de Gaulle in the months before Khrushchev's visit to France could hardly have been more cordial. Khrushchev expressed his appreciation of the position de Gaulle and Prime Minister Debré had taken vis-à-vis the frontiers of Germany and commended de Gaulle on his decision to let the Algerian people determine their own destiny. The Soviet leader stressed the fact that close historical ties existed between France and Algeria and that cooperation between the two peoples could help establish peace in Algeria. If France could find a peaceful solution to the Algerian problem, the prestige of France would increase in the eyes of the world and her role as a world power would grow.

In a speech given on November 14, 1959, Khrushchev stressed that there were no conflicts of interest between France and the USSR. Although he admitted that de Gaulle differed with him on the solution to the German problem, the French president had no sympathy for German revisionism and recognized the existing borders of the two German states as final.

Khrushchev's visit to France, March 23 to April 3, 1960

Premier Khrushchev arrived in France on March 23 for talks with President de Gaulle. First, he would stay three days in Paris and visit the highlights of the city. Next, he would make a several-day tour of various French provinces and cities, where he would study French achievements in the fields of agriculture, science, and culture and meet representatives of various French economic and social groups. Finally, he would return to Paris for a series of meetings with President de Gaulle in Paris and at Rambouillet.

At these meetings, President de Gaulle stressed the necessity of an alliance among the great powers because of the grave nuclear risk. However, this alliance would be very difficult to undertake if any of the parties insisted on the solution of problems as complex as Germany and Berlin.

During Khrushchev's visit, de Gaulle made a speech in which he stressed that both France and Russia derived their origin from the same civilization and that both nations had been allies twice in recent history. Although at present France and Russia belonged to two different camps, declared de Gaulle, East-West relations had arrived at a point where it was necessary to do something so that rivalries would not lead to destruction. Khrushchev favored a relaxation of tensions between East and West but spoke about the "liquidation of the vestiges of the war," a solution to the German problem, and the question of West Berlin.

During these conversations at Rambouillet, France exploded her first atomic bomb in the Sahara. Although the USSR had formerly expressed her regret at this decision, the event did not strain the atmosphere of the meetings. President de Gaulle and Premier Khrushchev exchanged views on the problem of disarmament, and both men agreed that disarmament was the most important and most urgent problem of the age. They expressed the hope that the meetings among the ten powers then taking place in Geneva would result in defining some points of agreement on the question of general and complete disarmament under a workable international system of controls.[5]

The representatives of both France and the USSR affirmed the need for increased contacts between the two. President de Gaulle and Premier Khrushchev noted with satisfaction the increased Franco-Soviet trade that had developed in the past few years, and a two-year trade agreement was concluded providing for reciprocal imports and exports. The two men also agreed to an increase in exchanges in the field of scientific research and the peaceful uses of atomic energy.

In a press conference given on April 2, the day before Premier Khrushchev left France, de Gaulle said that he did not wish to present the West with an ultimatum on the German question and thus risk a rupture in East-West relations at the summit conference. He would rather discuss other subjects such as disarmament at the summit talks. The German problem could be deferred to a future meeting.

On his return to Moscow, Khrushchev said that the meetings at Rambouillet had been important and useful. If the USSR and France, two great powers of Europe, united their efforts with all

other countries, pronouncing themselves for peace, it would be
an insurmountable obstacle for any nation to start a new war in
Europe.

In April, Charles de Gaulle visited the United States and gave
his impression of Nikita Khrushchev as a man with a strong personality who had fought all his life for his ideas, and as a symbol
and an expression of the Russia of today, not the Russia of yesterday or even the Russia of ten years ago.

Summary Conference of May 12-16, 1960

The summit conference that was held in Paris between May 12
and May, 16, 1960, among President Eisenhower, Prime Minister
Macmillan, President de Gaulle, and Premier Khrushchev took
place in an atmosphere very different from the one that had been
contemplated six months or even one month before.

In the interim between de Gaulle's meeting with Khrushchev
from March 23 to April 2 and the Paris Summit Conference of
May 12 through May 16, an unexpected incident had occurred
that was to dampen East-West relations for a number of months
to come. An American U-2 plane on a spy mission over Soviet
territory was shot down on May 1. Khrushchev decided to make
an international incident out of this unfortunate episode. He demanded that the conference not begin its work until President
Eisenhower explained why flights of observation over Russia were
taking place, and gave an apology as well. Since Eisenhower
would not bend to Khrushchev's demand for an apology,
Khrushchev did not appear at the meetings of the Four which
de Gaulle took the initiative to convoke. Khrushchev left Paris
after having made declarations to the press on the gravity of the
situation created by the U-2 incident.[6] He asked for the ad-
journment of the trip President Eisenhower was getting ready to
make to the USSR and formulated the theses of his government
on grave problems dividing East and West. Among them were
the problem of a German peace treaty and the question of Berlin,
the two issues he had soft-pedaled only two months before at
Rambouillet.

In what was probably the most emotional speech he ever gave,
President de Gaulle said on May 31, 1960, in a nationwide radio-
television address that the U-2 incident did not constitute sufficient motive to refuse to discuss world issues. He felt it excessive

of Khrushchev to demand public apologies and reparations from Washington since the plane had been shot down and its films held. Moreover, a guarantee had been given that such an incident would not occur again. "At the very moment when Moscow has launched a new space vehicle passing over the West eighteen times a day, such a demand seems a little excessive," he concluded.[7]

The division of the peoples that inhabit Europe and North America is the gravest evil of our times. Two camps have been set up face to face, and it depends on Moscow and Washington whether most of humanity will or will not be wiped out within several hours. In such a situation de Gaulle felt that no ideological argument or disagreement was important in comparison with the necessity of exorcising this peril. Therefore, he made three proposals in an attempt to prevent a nuclear holocaust: a détente or bettering of international relations by putting an end to provocative speeches and actions, by increasing trade, cultural exchanges, and tourism; a controlled disarmament; cooperation between East and West whereby both would devote themselves to the service of mankind, help in the progress of underdeveloped peoples, and collaborate on great projects of scientific research.

De Gaulle stressed that France had always had sympathy for the peoples of the USSR and Central Europe and hoped to see the iron curtain that separated her from her traditional allies lifted.[9]

Although France hoped for peace, disarmament, and détente, until these were achieved, she had to be ready to defend herself. She had to acquire nuclear armaments since others had them, and her destiny, although associated with that of her allies, had to be in her own hands.

Thus May, 1960, came to an end and with it the period of détente, which had lasted one year. The world was about to enter an uncertain tomorrow.

CHAPTER 5

The Period of Deterioration in Franco-Soviet Relations

THE period between the failure of the Paris Summit Conference of May, 1960, and the end of 1963 was a time in which friction between France and the USSR increased. The failure of the summit conference opened an era of crises in East-West relations for the next two and a half years that climaxed in the Cuban missile crisis. Although a less tense situation existed between East and West after the Cuban missile crisis of October, 1962, Franco-Soviet relations throughout the following year remained strained because of the Franco-German Accord and the failure of France to sign the Nuclear Test Ban (Moscow) Treaty of 1963.

The period between the failure of the Paris Summit Conference and the Kennedy-Khrushchev meeting of June, 1961, was one of violent polemics between France and the USSR on colonial questions, Algeria, disarmament, and Germany. On June 2, 1960, Premier Khrushchev addressed new proposals on disarmament to the West and placed them before the Committee of Ten in Geneva. In a message sent to Nikita Khrushchev on June 10, President de Gaulle expressed the French point of view on disarmament, which differed in several respects from the Soviet proposal of June 2.

In a new message dated June 26, Khrushchev reproached de Gaulle for having gone back on the ideas he had expressed at Rambouillet less than three months before. Khrushchev stated that de Gaulle had suggested that nuclear disarmament begin with the destruction of the vehicles of nuclear armament (rockets), a suggestion with which Khrushchev was in full agreement at Rambouillet. But, according to Khrushchev, the French government subsequently changed its attitude and substituted control of nuclear armaments for destruction. Khrushchev's message indicated that, because of the general attitude of the West toward disarmament, it would no longer be possible for the USSR to participate in the Committee of Ten in Geneva, and he proposed to submit the question to the General Assembly of the United Nations, where it might receive a better reception.

Charles de Gaulle replied on June 30 that the French position on disarmament had not changed one iota. He realized that whereas it was difficult to control the elimination of all nuclear stockpiles then in existence, it was more practical to oversee the prohibition (interdiction) of transport of nuclear charges by rockets and planes capable of delivering them. France felt that it was not only necessary but also possible to control this interdiction.

On July 23, Khrushchev again charged that there had been a change in the French position on disarmament and again belittled the work of the Committee of Ten in Geneva. De Gaulle's answer to Khrushchev, which came on August 22, reaffirmed the position he had taken on June 30 and disagreed that the interest of disarmament would best be served by a debate before such a heterogeneous body of nations as the UN.

The misunderstanding between de Gaulle and Khrushchev over disarmament may well have been sincere. The scientific jargon is so complex that even a well-educated person finds difficulty in understanding it when it is explained to him in his own language. When one takes into account that de Gaulle spoke no Russian and Khrushchev no French, both men might well have mistakenly believed that they were in accord on disarmament at Rambouillet.

The summer of 1960 was tumultuous in the field of East-West relations. The Soviet Union and the West opposed each other in the United Nations' debate over the Congo. As the United States began to send more troops to Laos, and Cuba began to expel American business from the country, Soviet-American relations hit a new low. De Gaulle did not agree with the American belief that the West should respond to the pressure of Communist forces in Laos. He was adamant in his belief that the Laotians were struggling for their national identity and that it would be a grave error for the West to intervene.

Tass accused France of participating in a colonial plot to stifle the national liberation movement of the people, a plot of which one of the links in the chain of aggression was the Congo. In September, Khrushchev, while participating in the opening session of the General Assembly of the UN, attacked the politics of the

West in the Congo, the remainder of Africa, and the Middle East, and proposed a resolution on the total liquidation of colonialism.

Soviet Criticism of French Politics in Algeria

Moscow went back on Khrushchev's statement at Rambouillet relating to France's concern for the Algerian people. On July 31, Tass criticized the bloody colonial war in Algeria, while *Pravda* acknowledged that although de Gaulle had presented a series of proposals on Algeria, there was always a demand at their base for an unconditional capitulation of the Algerian Liberation Movement. *Pravda* accused the French government of failing to have meaningful talks on a peaceful solution to the Algerian affair, and President de Gaulle of leading the Algerian problem to a dead end. In a speech before the Supreme Soviet in the fall of 1960, Foreign Minister Andrei Gromyko said that just as Hitler was unable to suppress France, all attempts by France to smash the Algerian National Liberation Movement would end in failure.

France reacted strongly to these attacks, likening the nature of Soviet power over the various ethnic regions of the USSR and Eastern Europe associated with the USSR to Western colonialism. In a statement in October at Chambéry de Gaulle said: "France will not accept for its law a dictum by a conjuncture of states that are more or less totalitarian and professionals in dictatorship and newly born states."[1] At Nice in late October, he delivered a more direct attack. He spoke of a hard and dangerous world:

It is that in particular and even so to speak uniquely because of this empire whose name you know and which intends not only to keep under its yoke the peoples which already at the time of the tsars were annexed to it and then afterwards were reannexed and again disfigured but also to oppress a certain number of nations of Europe: Poland, Czechoslovakia, Hungary, Rumania, Bulgaria, Albania, Estonia, Latvia, Lithuania, Prussia and Saxony. I hope for their sake that I have not forgotten any of them. This same power, this same empire intends today to intervene in a matter which we must settle: the Algerian question.[2]

On November 10, *Pravda* accused de Gaulle of turning his attention away from the true causes of his failure in Algeria to lies about the USSR. He was accused of talking in unison with American propaganda. On December 31, de Gaulle hoped that order and progress would prevail in the new states of Africa "despite the Soviet Empire which, not content to colonize 40 million Asiatic Moslems and Caucasians, to enslave a good dozen of peoples who are complete strangers to it, encourages and exploits all political agitations in order to gain a foothold in troubled countries."[3]

The German Problem

Moscow still hoped that Germany and Berlin would be discussed at a new summit conference that could be held if Kennedy were elected and took office as President of the United States in January, 1961. However, after the American election of November, 1960, Khrushchev seemed more favorably disposed to a Soviet-American meeting than to a summit conference. Soviet criticism of the United States subsided temporarily but continued toward Paris because of the consolidation of ties between Paris and Bonn. The USSR reproached France for closing her eyes to the rebirth of German militarism and the revisionist policies of the German Federal Republic. Since France had agreed to allow a certain number of German troops on her soil, the Soviet press accused France of getting ready to put French soil at the disposition of the German militarists and of conceding to the German armed forces the use of French bases.

At the Kennedy-Khrushchev meeting of June, 1961, in Vienna, Khrushchev repeated to Kennedy his well-known threat—that if the West refused to conclude a peace treaty with the two German states and evacuate the city of West Berlin, the USSR would sign a separate peace treaty with the German Democratic Republic, ending the rights of the Western powers in Berlin and conferring upon the East German authorities control of all communications between West Germany and West Berlin. Moreover, Khrushchev set a deadline of December 31, 1961, by which date the Western powers must be out of Berlin. Thus, a new Berlin crisis was created.

President de Gaulle recommended that the West react firmly to this new Soviet threat, and in a radio-television address of July 12 he told the Soviet leaders that if they wanted détente and coexistence, they should stop their menacing tactics. He said that

the rulers of the USSR had started the Berlin crisis not only because of internal difficulties within their own country but also because of the attitudes of the peoples of Eastern Europe. The
crisis had been started in order to take the eyes of the peoples of
the USSR and Eastern Europe off domestic affairs and a low
standard of living and onto the so-called German danger. De
Gaulle went on to say that it was not true that the totalitarian
camp was militarily stronger than the West. A world conflict
would be a disaster for all, he declared. This fact the Soviet leaders know he concluded, in spite of all of their boasting.[4] President de Gaulle stressed above all that even if the USSR could obtain local advantages from the Berlin crisis, the West could retaliate against the USSR from bases all over the world.

The Soviet leaders did not appear at all apprehensive about
this speech at first, and on August 13 Soviet authorities undertook the construction of the Berlin Wall, which physically sealed
off the two sectors of the city, preventing East Berliners from es-
caping to the West. The reason for Khrushchev's intensification of
the Berlin crisis is a little obscure. According to the speculation
of one scholar of Soviet foreign policy, "Perhaps it was pressure
from the Chinese to adopt a more aggressive attitude toward the
West, an effort to exploit Western preoccupation with Laos and
the Congo and American embarrassment over Castro's Communist Cuba, a desire to bolster the East German Regime by seal-
ing off the remaining escape route of East Germans to the West.
Or perhaps Khrushchev felt that after almost three years he had
to show something or face rising opposition among his Party
colleagues."[5]

De Gaulle immediately recalled a French unit from Algeria to
reinforce his military position in Germany. After Khrushchev's
bold move in August, he announced on October 17 at the
Twenty-second Communist Party Congress that he was renounc-
ing December 31 as the date he had previously fixed to sign a
peace treaty with East Germany in favor of a negotiated settlement. It seemed as if the hard line and united front the Western
powers were putting forth in Germany and Berlin was resulting
in a backing off by the Soviet leaders, but not a backing down.

President de Gaulle was cool to the idea of negotiations with
Moscow, since Soviet threats had not entirely disappeared. He
feared that the leaders of the USSR might interpret any conces-

sion by the Western leaders to negotiate as a sign of weakness on their part. He feared that any meeting between the USSR and the Western powers vis-à-vis Berlin and Germany at this time would have an unhappy ending, and declared on December 29, 1961: "Any negotiations which might take place between the Western powers and Soviet Russia to try to regulate the problems of the world, notably that of Germany, would have without doubt our constructive participation, but it would be necessary first to stop the tension created by the threats and menaces of the Kremlin. It would also be necessary that these negotiations try to rebalance Europe, not aggravate the hold of Moscow on our continent."[6]

On February 5, 1962, de Gaulle expressed his feelings about a meeting between the Soviet Union and the West even more vividly: "By taking the role of neither negotiating on Berlin or Germany as long as the Soviet Union shall not have ceased its threats and its demands and shall not have created a situation of true international détente, we feel that we have avoided for our allies and for ourselves either catastrophic retreat or dramatic rupture or a tragi-comic engulfment, to which end this conference would have come."[7]

De Gaulle, a man of deep perception, realized that the West had absolutely nothing to gain from a meeting with the Soviet Union over Berlin and Germany and much to lose. Since the status of East Berlin was not in question but only that of West Berlin, the most the West could hope to gain in attending such a meeting was the granting of only a few concessions to the USSR on Berlin. At worst, a real tragedy could emerge if Khrushchev were to sense any weaknesses among Western leaders and insist upon all his demands. In such an eventuality, the West would either have to give in and surrender millions of West Berliners to the mercy of totalitarians or remain adamant and face the possibility of a real crisis in Berlin.

In spite of de Gaulle's warning, talks took place between Foreign Minister Andrei Gromyko and the American ambassador in Moscow in the early weeks of 1962 and were followed by meetings between Gromyko and Dean Rusk in Geneva during the month of March. Then in April and May talks were held in Washington, D.C., between Rusk and Dobrynin, the Soviet ambassador to the United States.

For reasons unforeseen at the time, these talks were not destined to get off the ground. It was a stroke of good fortune for the West. East-West tensions eased for several months only to erupt with the dramatic events in October, 1962, in Cuba, after which, for reasons that historians can only speculate about, the Berlin question was temporarily shelved by Khrushchev. Hindsight again proves de Gaulle's intuition correct. The Western world owes a great debt to his stubbornness with regard to top-level talks on Berlin and Germany and to his attitude of wait and see. In 1964, when the Soviet Union signed a treaty of friendship and mutual assistance with the German Democratic Republic, the status quo in West Berlin was reaffirmed much to the chagrin of the Pankow regime. Then, in the summer of that year, Khrushchev shocked the East German authorities by accepting an invitation to visit the German Federal Republic in the fall, a trip he was destined never to make. Khrushchev was ousted in September, 1964, and his successors didn't raise the question of the status of Berlin.

Franco-Soviet Incident over Algeria

There was to be one last Franco-Soviet incident over Algeria—one that was unnecessary because it came on the eve of Algerian independence. Yet it almost led to a break in diplomatic relations between France and the USSR.

The Evian Accords, which were signed on March 18, 1962, between France and the provisional government of Algeria (G.P.R.A.), granted independence to Algeria, provided that both a majority of Frenchmen in metropolitan France and a majority of Algerians voted for this status in referenda soon to be held. There was never any doubt that the Algerians would approve these accords and little doubt that the French would approve them. But between the time that the accords were signed and before either referendum, the USSR recognized the provisional government of Algeria. Technically, French sovereignty had not yet ended in Algeria, since the referenda had not taken place. The French foreign minister was infuriated that the USSR had given *de jure* recognition to the G.P.R.A. and proposed to establish diplomatic relations with Algeria.

On March 19, the Soviet ambassador in Paris, Mr. Vinogradov, was summoned by the French foreign minister, Maurice Couve de Murville, and told that the cease-fire in Algeria had not modified the status of the country and that France was continuing to exercise internal and external sovereignty over Algeria at least until the referenda. Furthermore, the USSR had been warned against taking the step that she had just taken, and such a gesture on the part of the USSR could not fail to have damaging effects on Franco-Soviet relations. Mr. Vinogradov was then compelled to ask his government for an explanation.

This event led to a new encounter between Couve de Murville and Vinogradov on March 23. Upon being informed by the Soviet ambassador that his government had no intention of going back on its decision to recognize the G.P.R.A., the French foreign minister replied that the maintenance of Franco-Soviet diplomatic relations on the ambassadorial level had become impossible. Mr. Dejean, the French ambassador in Moscow, was then recalled, and the Soviet government was compelled to recall Vinogradov.

The USSR was not belligerent at this point over the Algerian issue, knowing that it would be just a matter of weeks before Algerian independence became a reality. The Soviet press published a declaration that stressed the fact that the Evian Accords dealt not only with the cease-fire in Algeria but with political, military, economic, and cultural relations between France and an independent Algeria. This relationship proved that France herself almost recognized the provisional government as the authorized representative of the Algerian people. The declaration went on to state that Soviet recognition of the G.P.R.A. meant no ill intent toward France and recalled that the USSR had always stated in the past that a negotiated settlement in Algeria would conform to the best interests of France and Algeria.

The incident had short-range repercussions on Franco-Soviet relations. Even though an overwhelming majority of Frenchmen in metropolitan France voted in favor of the Evian Accords in a nationwide referendum on April 8, 1962, and 99 percent of the people of Algeria voted in favor of these accords on July 1, resulting in the independence of Algeria and the exchange of ambassadors between France and Algeria on July 3, the Franco-Soviet ambassadors were absent from their respective posts until the end of July. The USSR did not send an ambassador to Algeria during this entire period, but after diplomatic relations between

France and the USSR were restored at the ambassadorial level and the situation had calmed down, Moscow and Algeria exchanged representatives.

De Gaulle and Disarmament

In 1961, the United States and the Soviet Union made an accord on the creation of a Committee of Eighteen charged with examining the problem of disarmament. This committee consisted of representatives from five Western, five Communist, and eight neutral countries. Khrushchev proposed that discussions open with the participation of representatives at the highest level from the member nations, a kind of summit conference on disarmament. He underlined the danger of continuing nuclear tests.

France refused to participate in these discussions. On February 12, 1962, President de Gaulle, in response to Premier Khrushchev, expressed his desire to take part in meaningful negotiations that could offer the world even modest hope in the direction of nuclear disarmament. But de Gaulle did not believe that a ban on nuclear testing would lead to disarmament, since some nations had already accumulated stockpiles of nuclear arms. He again proposed the destruction, interdiction, and control of the vehicles of nuclear arms.

Khrushchev answered de Gaulle on February 27 and asserted that countries that did not possess nuclear arms also had an interest in the question of disarmament. Their participation in the conference would be useful in maintaining contacts with nations that did have nuclear arms. He criticized France's attitude of refusal to participate in the Conference of Eighteen as a negative attitude vis-à-vis the regulation of an international problem.

Franco-German Rapprochement

As early as 1958, the USSR claimed that it favored a Franco-German rapprochement between a democratic France and a democratic Germany. This statement was so ambiguous that one can lend any meaning he likes to it. One can interpret it to mean that the USSR would favor a rapprochement between the peoples of France and the peoples of Germany, but even this statement lends itself to more than one meaning. "Peoples" in Soviet terminology means the toiling masses, the proletariat.

In July, 1962, Chancellor Adenauer visited Paris for talks with

President de Gaulle, and in September President de Gaulle visited Bonn. Moscow commented that the talks between the two men left no doubt that any entente that ensued between Adenauer and de Gaulle would serve to exacerbate the international situation. It was not a question of friendship between the French and the German peoples, Moscow explained, but between the rulers of France and those of Germany, who wished to reexamine the consequences of World War II. It was called the Paris-Bonn Axis against the USSR and her allies. On September 11, Tass said that de Gaulle was now far from the realistic judgment he had maintained after World War II on the threat of German militarism, and again asserted that a peace treaty should be concluded with the two German states, normalizing the situation in West Berlin.

The situation in the summer of 1962, after the visit of Adenauer to Paris but before the visit of de Gaulle to Bonn in September, was tense. There were many incidents concerning the obstruction of routes between West Germany and West Berlin by Soviet authorities. Many citizens experienced delays of several hours in attempts to enter West Berlin upon their approach to the city. The Soviet Command in Berlin declared the quadripartite agreement out of date, and Moscow expressed the hope that the West would take up conversations on the liquidation of the Berlin crisis in the near future.

The events in Cuba in October, 1962, led to another crossroad in East-West relations. Although France was not directly affected by the Cuban missile crisis, President de Gaulle made it quite clear that he was in agreement with President Kennedy on the handling of this incident.

After the Cuban missile crisis had subsided, both the Western camp and the Soviet bloc made a reappraisal of their relations with each other. The Berlin crisis faded into the background as a verbal tirade began between the USSR and Communist China over many problems, including Khrushchev's backdown in Cuba. These diverse elements were to influence Franco-Soviet relations for some time to come.

A Better Year in Franco-Soviet Relations

The settlement of the Algerian question in July, 1962, had removed one of the major sources of friction between the USSR and France. Although the decrease in tension between East and West that followed the Cuban missile crisis was another element favorable to the amelioration of Franco-Soviet relations, the Franco-German Treaty of January 22, 1963, and de Gaulle's negative attitude toward the Nuclear Test Ban Treaty that same year continued to dampen, yet only slightly, relations between the two countries throughout the year.

The Franco-German Treaty of Cooperation of January 22, 1963, provided for consultations between the two countries on defense, foreign policy, and cultural affairs. The USSR reacted negatively. The treaty occasioned the sending by the Soviet government of an official note to President de Gaulle on February 5, according to which the Soviet government viewed the new Franco-German Treaty as a narrow political-military alliance which would only serve in the end to increase international tension. The treaty, according to Soviet authorities,

is an outrage since the Big Four assumed in 1945 the obligation of extirpating German and Nazi militarism once and for all.

. . . One searches in vain for anything in that treaty which has as its aim the solution of important international problems such as disarmament, nondissemination of nuclear arms, a German peace. Instead one finds clauses that provide for the stationing of French and German troops on each other's soil, coordination of activities of military research, the exchange of professors and students of the military establishment. France has signed a new politico-military accord with a nation which stands for the revision of its territorial frontiers. Does France not know the political and military aims of those who govern the GFR? France has arrived at an entente with the revanchist forces of West Germany. This treaty means that French troops are on hand to fight for West German militarists; that means that France will fight for the revision of the results of World War II. The President of France has recently put himself on record as saying (on January 14) in a press conference that Germany must decide for herself what kind of nuclear arms she wants. If that is France's attitude, one may ask, of what value are the declarations of the French government on the subject of its attachment to the cause of peace and diminution of tension in Europe.

. . . The USSR cannot understand France's policy toward Germany in the light of statements made by General de Gaulle after the war. It is France's own affair to choose her friends. But when France chooses as her friend a nation that calls the USSR its worst and mortal enemy simply because the USSR is pledged to prevent the revision of German frontiers, then one quickly perceives what that friendship means.

. . . This is not a treaty of peace but a treaty of war that has been signed.[8]

The French government replied to the Soviet note on March 30. The reply stressed that the USSR, whose power was being revealed each day by the declarations of its directors, could not seriously feel itself menaced by a treaty that did not in any way change the military conditions in Europe. The note stated that the treaty was a defensive one. It was in the interest of all governments to see France and Germany engaged in close cooperation, which could only contribute to serve peaceful interests in Europe. The note concluded:

The French government takes up with interest that the Soviet government invokes the obligations assumed in common at the end of the war by the four powers with regard to Germany. These obligations impose on each of the interested governments the duty to do nothing that might compromise the perspectives of a final solution of the German problem, founded on the respect of the right of auto-determination and conforming to the demands of security of all. The French government is conscious that the treaty of January 22, 1963, is entirely compatible with these principles.[9]

The Soviet government answered the French note on May 17. After pointing out that France's decision to give herself nuclear arms was showing the way to the German Federal Republic, it went on to stress the need for cooperation:

The foreign political activities of the USSR serve the noble cause of reinforcing peace and friendship between peoples. If the Franco-German Treaty did serve the cause of peace, it would only encounter sustenance from the USSR.
. . . This treaty is military in scope. If the treaty had concerned itself with a mutual spiritual enrichment between the two peoples, opened new possibilities for cooperation in the political, economic, scientific domain, facilitated rapport between the two countries or even regulated other problems touching the interest of both countries, but this military treaty gives the GFR privileges she does not even have in NATO.
The whole foreign policy of the GFR has but one aim: to take revenge from the war she has lost. The leaders of West Germany realize that they cannot attain their aims without outside assistance. The military circles of West Germany therefore look for partners in order that their aims may be realized.

. . . The Soviet government wants to call the attention of the French government to the fact that the Franco-German Treaty and the consequences flowing from its execution raise grave questions relative to the perspective of developing Franco-Soviet relations. By making this treaty the basis of her foreign policy, France is playing with the forces that do not permit the development of Franco-Soviet relations.

Geography and history have made France and Russia natural allies. . . . If France and the USSR, being the two largest European powers on the continent, could agree on essential questions upon which European peace depends, no force would be strong enough to change the map of Europe. Friendly rapports between the USSR and France could become the link that would unite Eastern and Western Europe and greatly aid the insaturation of a peaceful cooperation between nations.[10]

It seems that this Soviet note was playing upon de Gaulle's idea of a Europe from the Atlantic to the Urals, a free confederation of European nations with close cultural, social, and economic links, pursuing policies in conformity with each other. Actually, what Moscow feared most was that in a Paris-Bonn entente, Bonn would soon become the dominating element because of its economic superiority, industrial potential, and manpower.

Moscow's fears were short-lived, for about the time of the second Soviet note to France on the Franco-German Treaty, complications began to develop between France and the German Federal Republic. Just before the treaty was signed by President de Gaulle and Chancellor Adenauer on January 22, the former had vetoed British entry into the Common Market, which the other five members favored. As a result, the German Bundestag attached a preamble to the treaty emphasizing its support for British entrance into the Common Market. Only after this preamble was attached did the Bundestag agree to the ratification of the treaty. The preamble irked de Gaulle, and within a very short time Franco-German relations turned somewhat sour.

Adenauer retired as chancellor of the German Federal Republic at the age of eighty-six immediately after signing the treaty with de Gaulle. Although he had hoped that this treaty would be the "grand finale" of his career, it seemed as if neither his successor, Ludwig Erhard, nor the German people wanted to weaken their country's ties with Great Britain and the United States. The treaty was based on the assumption that West Germany should accept French rather than American leadership and protection. Within a short time de Gaulle was to remark that this was not the only treaty that had faded as quickly as a rose.[11]

With the independence of Algeria and the souring of Franco-German relations, the door to the improvement of Franco-Soviet relations was opened. De Gaulle's intransigence on the cessation of nuclear tests above the atmosphere did not prove to be a substantial barrier to improved relations between the two countries.

To the treaty forbidding nuclear experiments above the surface of the earth, signed in Moscow on July 5, 1963, by the United States, Great Britain, the USSR, and numerous other countries, neither France nor Communist China lent their signatures. France received more criticism from her American and British allies for refusing to sign the treaty than she encountered from the Kremlin. Surprisingly, Moscow's attacks against the French government were at most moderate, while the harshest attacks were reserved for West Germany. Even though the German Federal Republic had signed the Moscow Treaty, the Soviet government accused her of aspiring to the access of nuclear arms by means of the multilateral forces of NATO, of using her efforts to stop not only progress toward East-West agreements on disarmament but also to impede the reduction of military forces and other measures of security in Europe. Although there might have been some truth in these Soviet charges, to any objective observer they were highly exaggerated. After all, it was France, not West Germany, that refused to sign the treaty.

In his press conference in Paris on July 29, de Gaulle was asked to give his opinion of the recently concluded agreement on the banning of nuclear tests above the surface of the earth. His position was very clear. He expressed joy that the USSR, the United States, and Great Britain had decided to halt their nuclear tests in space, the air, and the sea. De Gaulle felt that all three countries had already carried out these tests hundreds of times and that it was difficult to see what purpose new tests could serve. But such a promise to ban nuclear tests above the earth's surface had no meaning for small countries that did not possess nuclear weapons and did not intend to manufacture them. France, which was far behind the USSR, the United States, and Great Britain in her testing of nuclear weapons, would be put at a disadvantage by signing such an agreement.[12]

Then de Gaulle went on to criticize the agreement and said that it did not ban the testing of nuclear weapons beneath the surface of the earth. Both camps had the means to annihilate the world. This treaty did not prevent either side from manufacturing missiles, rockets, airplanes, submarines, and satellites. Since the savings they made from halting these tests would enable them to build more weapons of destruction, the Moscow Treaty could have only limited importance. De Gaulle emphasized that if the United States and the Soviet Union were to reach the point of disarmament where they agreed to the destruction, interdiction, and control of the vehicles of nuclear arms, France would gladly subscribe to such a treaty. Unfortunately, he continued, nothing indicated that such a point was about to be reached.[13]

De Gaulle ended by saying that he would propose to the three other atomic powers some initial effective disarmament measures in the near future. A mere agreement between nations already invested with immeasurable power and those that did not possess this power would only continue to strengthen the hegemonies of the Soviets and the Anglo-Saxons. This agreement would not prevent France from equipping herself with the means already possessed by the Soviets and the Anglo-Saxons. If France were to sign such an agreement, her own independence and security would never again belong to her.[14]

After the signing of the Treaty of Moscow, the United States and Great Britain agreed to examine with their allies a conclusion of a pact of nonaggression between members of NATO and of the Warsaw Pact. De Gaulle expressed his opinion of the Non-Aggression Pact on July 29, 1963:

As for the project of a nonaggression pact about which they have, so they say, talked to Moscow, between states which are part of NATO and those which are subjected to the yoke of the Kremlin, I must say immediately that France does not appreciate this assimilation between the Atlantic Alliance and Communist servitude. And also, moreover, there is no need for any pact for France to declare that she will never be the first to attack, being understood that she would defend herself with all means at her disposal against whoever would attack either her or her allies. But, today, she solemnly declares that there will never be French aggression. Therefore, there is no point in France's joining a nonaggression pact.[15]

De Gaulle was disturbed that the United States, Britain, and the USSR had begun to discuss "European questions in the absence of Europeans" in Moscow after the signing of the Treaty of Moscow. He was referring to the exclusion of France from these talks, since her representatives were not in Moscow to sign the treaty.

By the summer of 1963, de Gaulle was ready for improved relations with the USSR. The Cuban affair and the signing of the Treaty of Moscow triggered the dispute between Red China and the Soviet Union to a point it had never before reached, and Moscow's allies in Eastern Europe began to take an attitude of greater autonomy toward the Russians. The USSR was searching for a détente on her western borders, and France was becoming more and more the nation to which the USSR could turn, since Algeria was no longer a barrier to improved Franco-Soviet relations and the Franco-German Treaty did not turn out to entail the type of Franco-German cooperation the Soviets had feared.

By the end of 1963, de Gaulle was getting ready to denounce the two hegemonies, Soviet and American, over Europe and the world. France continued to think of the United States as her ally but not as her commander in chief. The theme of France was going to be that the United States and the USSR should not intervene in the affairs of others. But what did de Gaulle have in mind at this point? He realized that although the USSR might be ready to relax her hold on Eastern Europe, she would never willingly relinquish this area as her sphere of influence. If the United States withdrew her forces from Western Europe, a power vacuum would be created.

De Gaulle was a man who undoubtedly thought of foreign policy in long-range terms. A détente between East and West might eventually lead to a situation where both alliances could be dissolved. The United States would withdraw from Western Europe and the USSR from Eastern Europe. Under these circumstances, the Soviet Union might very well consent to the reunification of Germany up to the Oder and Neisse rivers. Germany as well as Eastern and Southeastern Europe would be demilitarized, leaving France and the USSR the only two nuclear powers in Europe. Thus, Western Europe might well become a sort of French sphere of influence, in which the various nations would accept the political leadership of France, while Eastern Europe would remain a Soviet sphere of influence. Since the balance of power would be tipped in favor of the Soviet Union under such an arrangement, France would have to maintain an alliance with the United States and Great Britain, who would act as the guarantors.

CHAPTER 6

The Period of Amelioration in Franco-Soviet Relations

THE year of 1963 came to an end and with it many of the differences that had plagued Franco-Soviet relations in the past. The German question seemed to be the only area in which France and the USSR disagreed basically, and the Soviet government was no longer insistent on the diplomatic recognition of the two German states and the evacuation of West Berlin by the allies. Although France's refusal to sign the Nuclear Test Ban Treaty created some discord between the two countries, the Soviet government did not consider France's determination to set up a nuclear force of her own an obstacle to good relations. De Gaulle's policy of decolonization suppressed the source of considerable irritation on the part of the USSR; and even the Soviet Press, which continued to stress neocolonialism in Africa, refrained from applying its attacks to France.

The year 1964 was marked by an amelioration of Franco-Soviet relations, but it was not until 1965 that a genuine rapprochement between the two countries ensued.

De Gaulle had already decided to establish full-fledged diplomatic relations with Communist China at the end of 1963, and on January 27, 1964, ambassadors between the two countries were exchanged. Even though Sino-Soviet relations were far from good at the time, the Soviet press described the decision of Paris to recognize Peking as a realistic one that would contribute to the amelioration of the international situation.

France and Russia decided to increase their commercial ties early in 1964, and in January of that year, Giscard d'Estaing, then the French finance minister, journeyed to Moscow to discuss the possibility of an increase in commercial exchanges. The USSR was interested in purchasing French equipment for the chemical industry, which the Soviets had decided to expand. The conversations between Giscard d'Estaing and the Soviet economists were cordial; and the following month Roudniev, the vice-president of the Soviet Scientific and Technical Council, made a trip to France to discuss commercial exchanges with France in the scientific and technical fields.

A Soviet parliamentary delegation headed by Nikolai Podgorny journeyed to France in late February and early March. The fact that this delegation was headed by a member of the Presidium of the Central Committee of the Communist Party of the USSR was indicative of the importance the Soviet government attached to this mission. Podgorny visited several large cities in France and met not only with Foreign Minister Couve de Murville and Prime Minister Pompidou but with President de Gaulle as well.

In an interview with the French press, Podgorny stressed the realistic attitude the French government had taken with regard to international problems and his feeling that Franco-Soviet cooperation had entered a new and positive phase of development. He praised de Gaulle for recognizing the principle of peaceful coexistence among countries with differing socioeconomic systems and pleaded for closer Franco-Soviet ties in the political, economic, and cultural spheres. Podgorny expressed his approval of France's realistic attitude toward China and extended an open invitation to Charles de Gaulle on behalf of Premier Khrushchev to visit the USSR whenever he chose.

By the end of March, Aleksei I. Adzhubei, editor of *Izvestia*, was in France for the signing of an agreement between the USSR and France on cultural exchanges. The Soviet Union was watching the development of de Gaulle's policy of independence within the Atlantic Alliance very carefully. Adzhubei found praiseworthy de Gaulle's views on Western Europe and his reaffirmation that the frontiers set by World War II should not be subject to change.[1] Russia opposed the proposal of a multilateral nuclear force in NATO, since it tended to move West Germany a step closer to a restoration of her military power. De Gaulle opposed this force, since he did not wish to relinquish to any international organization the right to make decisions of this type on behalf of France.

Franco-Soviet Declaration on Amelioration of Relations

A Franco-Soviet rapprochement began to manifest itself toward the end of the summer of 1964 in a series of Franco-Soviet declarations. The first was to be consecrated on the twentieth anniversary of the liberation of Paris (August 24). Premier Khrushchev, in a message to President de Gaulle, reminded him of the necessity of a Franco-Soviet responsibility for the security of Europe. De Gaulle, in his answer of September 1, spoke of the courageous struggle of the Soviet people during World War II and the need for friendship between the two countries.

Even the removal of Nikita Khrushchev in September, 1964, did not seem to have an adverse effect on Franco-Soviet relations. The new Soviet leaders were even more intent than Khrushchev had been on broadening relations with France. Several weeks after Khrushchev's ouster, on the fortieth anniversary of the establishment of diplomatic relations between the USSR and France (October 27), *Pravda* praised France for her position on the German frontiers, the problems of Southeast Asia, and the United Nations, and commented that although the reasons for which the French and Soviet leaders had developed the same attitudes on these questions might differ, a real ground for cooperation between the two countries now existed. On the same day, Anastas Mikoyan, president of the Presidium of the Supreme Soviet (Soviet parliament), spoke of the importance of friendship, cooperation, and reciprocal aid between the two nations in the future.

De Gaulle responded in a telegram of October 29 that he was very touched to receive a greeting from the Soviet government on the fortieth anniversary of the establishment of diplomatic relations between the two countries and ended by saying: "During these forty years we have both traveled a long road and gone through terrible trials. We can also state that, in spite of historical accidents, our two countries are tied deeply by a durable friendship, by the conviction to retain a certain heritage and a reciprocal and cordial interest."[2]

A long-term commercial accord was signed between the two countries in October as a result of contacts that had started at the beginning of the year with Giscard d'Estaing's visit to the USSR and Roudniev's visit to France. French and Soviet ministers in Paris finished negotiating a new trade pact whereby France granted Russia seven-year credits for purchases of capital goods, despite West German and American opposition. France agreed to increase her purchases of Russian crude oil, and Russia agreed to double her purchases of capital goods from France to $140 million. A five-year trade agreement was to be signed in 1966, when the three-year trade agreement expired.[3]

Speaking before the Supreme Soviet on December 9, Aleksei Kosygin declared that the two most importrant powers of continental Europe assumed a great responsibility for European security and that he was very optimistic about the prospects for the future development of Franco-Soviet relations. De Gaulle's New Year's message of December 31, 1964, said that France would multiply her relations with the states of Eastern Europe so that they would orient themselves internally toward peace.

In articles published by *Izvestia* in January and February, 1965, the problem of European security was given more emphasis than usual. In March it proposed a general European security treaty, which had been advanced by the USSR several times in the past, and in addition a nonaggression pact between the members of NATO and those of the Warsaw Pact. It suggested that even West Germany, which had joined NATO in 1954 and assumed military obligations toward her Western allies, could assume these same obligations toward Eastern Europe as well in a new European security treaty.

De Gaulle's Press Conference
of February 4, 1965

After expressing his views on the UN and the international monetary problem, de Gaulle admitted in his press conference of February 4 that the German problem was still the biggest stumbling block to an accommodation between East and West. The division of Germany that resulted from World War II had been deepened by the Cold War. The economic and social prosperity of the German Federal Republic and the West German people's fear of communism prompted her to enter NATO. But the West could not promise unity to the German people short of engaging in a war with the USSR, and no nation was disposed to such a misadventure. De Gaulle indicated that the division of Germany was unnatural and could not be indefinitely continued. Germany must renounce the use of nuclear weapons as its price for unity, he declared. A real and lasting peace must be negotiated between East and West, because neither side wished to fight to impose its solution on Europe and the world. Therefore it would be necessary to settle these problems by an entente.

De Gaulle also felt that it was necessary for Russia to evolve in such a way that she could see her future not in terms of totalitarian restraint imposed upon herself and on others but in terms of progress accomplished in common by free people. De Gaulle made the meaning of this last sentence quite clear when he went on to say that the nations that Russia had made her satellites must one day play their role in a new Europe. The six states of Western Europe that have already organized the European Economic Community must also succeed in organizing themselves in the political realm and in the realm of defense, in order to render possible a new equilibrium in Europe. Last, he stated: "It is necessary that Europe, mother of modern civilization, establish herself from the Atlantic to the Urals in peace and in cooperation, in view of developing her great resources and in such a way as to play jointly with America, her daughter, the role which falls on her as far as the progress of two billion men who have great need of her is concerned. What a role Germany could play in this ambition of the world for the old continent rejuvenated!"[4]

Pravda responded to de Gaulle's press conference by commending him for his views on the UN and on the necessity of its return to the spirit of the founders of the charter and also for his realistic views on the international monetary problem. As far as European security was concerned, *Pravda* indicated that de Gaulle was correct in saying that the solution of the German problem must take into account the frontiers of the country and an accord with all of her neighbors; but it regretted that de Gaulle did not make reference to the two German states, maintaining that his attitude on this point lacked political realism. It also reproached de Gaulle for appearing to make the ideals expressed in his press conference dependent upon the evolution of the "socialist" countries into something in the likeness of the West.

Visit of Foreign Minister
Andrei Gromyko to Paris

Foreign Minister Andrei Gromyko visited Paris between April 25 and April 30, 1965, for talks with President Charles de Gaulle and other French leaders. Foreign Minister Couve de Murville said that France and the USSR would use the visit to discuss world problems. The French foreign minister admitted that French and Soviet positions were close on many international issues and farther apart on others.

Gromyko's visit to France was arranged after Premier Kosygin suggested in Moscow on December 1, 1964, that France and the USSR hold regular consultations, since their policies now converged on a number of issues. When the United States began to bomb North Vietnam early in 1965, de Gaulle started to deliver anti-American statements on the situation in Europe and Asia.[5]

The Kremlin decided not to hold talks with the United States under these circumstances and turned to France instead, deciding to purchase the French SECAM color television process in preference to the American RCA system. It also arranged for the Gromyko visit to France to discuss European and world problems with de Gaulle, rather than with President Johnson.

Immediately before Gromyko's visit, *La Nation* had published an article entitled "A New Turning Point in Franco-Soviet Relations." Several days before the visit, when de Gaulle received the credentials of the new Soviet ambassador to France, Mr. Zorin, he stressed that there were no opposing national interests between France and the USSR. Zorin was a specialist on Germany and Central Europe. His appointment as the new ambassador to France emphasized the importance that the German problem was given by Soviet leaders in their negotiations with France.

The USSR hoped to get as much support as possible from de Gaulle for a cease-fire and peace negotiations in Vietnam and a recognition by the French government of the German Democratic Republic. She wished to stress the common views of Paris and Moscow on such matters as the UN, disarmament, and opposition to American policies in Asia, Africa, and Latin America.[6] Last, the Soviet government hoped that this meeting would shake the unity of the West and give the impression that France and the USSR were drawing closer. For some time in the past de Gaulle had been stressing France's independence from American influence. The main Soviet objective was to eject the Americans from Europe.

De Gaulle wanted to show the world that France had again become a first-rate power with an independent foreign policy. He was opposed to bilateral agreements between Washington and

Moscow on behalf of East and West. By threatening to make a separate deal with the Russians, he was letting the United States know that she could not talk with Moscow on behalf of the entire West. De Gaulle had hoped that he could become the leader of a strong Western Europe in close collaboration with West Germany. After the death of Adenauer, Erhard played along more with the United States, and Franco-German relations began to deteriorate. Then de Gaulle turned to Moscow, but at the same time he continued his attempts to rally the other five Common Market nations to the acceptance of his version of European unity.[7] By criticizing the American policy in Vietnam, de Gaulle gained the respect of the Third World.

The atmosphere surrounding Gromyko's visit to France was cordial, even if at times the views of the two countries on major international problems were far apart. Both agreed that the paramount question was war or peace.At the end of the Gromyko visit, a Franco-Soviet communiqué was issued indicating that it appeared an entente existed between the two countries on certain major issues. The Soviet government extended an invitation to Couve de Murville to visit the USSR.

The communiqué mentioned four big international problems: Southeast Asia, European security, disarmament, and the United Nations. On Southeast Asia, both France and the USSR agreed that the Geneva Accords of 1954 should be carried out. On the U.N., both nations agreed on the necessity of returning to the original spirit and principles of the organization. On European security and disarmament, both countries felt that these problems must lead to an accord, even though the two countries were far from agreement on these two problems.

It seemed as if European security and problems in Southeast Asia had occupied the bulk of the time devoted to Gromyko's talks with de Gaulle and Couve de Murville. On Vietnam, they established an accord on the nature of an eventual rule and on the necessity of being able to resolve the problem directly. On European security, differences between the two countries rested on the question of German reunification and the problem of the German Democratic Republic. France still continued to disagree that two German states existed and implied that she would not recognize the GDR.

The visit of Gromyko to France was significant. It was a switch in Gaullist policies toward West Germany which brought France and the USSR closer together. For the first time a Franco-Soviet rapprochement stood a good chance of coming about.

In the past, the Kremlin had been more interested in improving relations with the United States. Khrushchev had been anxious to reach an agreement with the United States on disarmament. For de Gaulle such an agreement would have meant a revival of the Yalta spirit of leadership of the two superpowers, which he feared. But soon after Khrushchev was removed, the United States stepped up her intervention in Vietnam, and the new Soviet leaders did not seem to be interested in negotiations with the United States under these conditions. Instead, they turned to France.

Nobody was certain what game the Russians were playing. Russia had shown little interest in a Gaullist Europe in the past, because of her belief that it would be dominated from Bonn. This was also the reason the Russians had shown little interest in de Gaulle's battle against American hegemony. De Gaulle discovered that the basic flaw in his "Grand Design" was the assumption that he could keep West Germany the junior partner. The Franco-German Treaty was followed by a deterioration rather than an improvement in de Gaulle's relationship with Germany; and soon after its signing, he began to realize that it was not a safe basis for his foreign policy.[8]

At his press conference of February 4, 1965, de Gaulle began to reveal how he intended to prevent Germany from gaining the upper hand. As a price for reunification, Germany would have to accept the Oder and Neisse rivers as her eastern frontier and renounce the use of nuclear weapons. At that point, Russia began to listen, and the Soviet leaders decided to send Gromyko to Paris.

Only two years before, de Gaulle had said that it was up to the leaders of the German Federal Republic to decide whether or not it would be necessary to secure nuclear weapons for their country. Apparently, he had since come to the conclusion that his Europe from the Atlantic to the Urals could only come about if Germany and Eastern and Southeastern Europe became a demilitarized zone. The Soviet leaders were willing to play along a little with his "Grand Design." But in the meantime, they desperately tried to get de Gaulle to recognize the division of Germany. In these efforts, the Russians totally failed.

Between April, when Gromyko visited France, and October, when Couve de Murville visited the USSR, the two men met in Vienna on May 15 to celebrate the tenth anniversary of the signing of the Austrian Treaty and again in New York, when the new session of the United Nations convened in September.

These meetings were cordial. Both men opposed United States' involvement in Vietnam. France was opposed to the creation of a multilateral nuclear force in NATO, and the USSR declared herself against any form of nuclear arms direct or indirect for Germany.

On June 22, Zorin declared that the amelioration of Franco-Soviet relations was an historic and inevitable process. On July 13, *Izvestia* stated that the possibility of strengthening the peace in Europe already existed as a result of new Franco-Soviet dialogues. All nations, it said, should recognize as the basis for this peace the present frontiers in Europe and the division of Germany. Neither Germany should obtain nuclear weapons.

Immediately before Couve de Murville's visit to the USSR, *Izvestia* printed an article on October 26 explaining that one of the causes of the uncertainty in Europe over the years lay in the fact that for a long time France and the USSR had found themselves far apart on the major issues. Now Franco-Soviet cooperation had incited other European countries to adopt a positive attitude toward a rapprochement. *Izvestia* concluded that the climate of Franco-Soviet relations was beginning to exercise a more favorable influence, day by day, on both the international situation and that in Europe.

The Trip of Couve de Murville to the USSR, October 28 to November 2, 1965

Upon his arrival in Moscow, Couve de Murville declared that the establishment of new rapports between France and the USSR was a necessary condition for a European settlement. Murville was given a tour of the country, guided by Mrs. Furtseva, the minister of culture. At the Black Sea, he met and spoke with Premier Kosygin and President Mikoyan. In Moscow, he visited Party Secretary Brezhnev and had political discussions with Foreign Minister Gromyko.

At the end of his visit, Murville declared that relations between the two countries were good, and Gromyko stressed that

French and Soviet views coincided on a number of points. Concerning Southeast Aisa and the UN, the joint communiqué issued on November 2, at the end of the talks between the two foreign ministers, added nothing new to the communiqué issued on April 30, at the end of Gromyko's visit to France. However, in this latest round of discussions, European questions were given priority over Southeast Asia and the UN.

The two ministers noted with satisfaction that a tendency had been manifesting itself for some time toward the normalization of East-West relations on the European continent, giving hope for the establishment of a détente, which would create the conditions for rapprochement and cooperation among all nations of Europe.

With regard to bilateral Franco-Soviet relations, the communiqué was more specific than the earlier one, especially in the economic and cultural spheres. A mutual interest was expressed in developing exchanges in conformity to the long-term commercial accord signed in Paris on October 30, 1964, setting forth a harmonious development of exchanges for a period of five years. The communiqué took note of the Franco-Soviet Accord of March 22, 1965, pertaining to the Soviet purchase of the French color television process SECAM. The two ministers mentioned the recent meeting of French and Soviet experts in space research and expressed the desire of their governments to conclude an appropriate accord on Franco-Soviet cooperation in this domain.[9]

The communiqué stated that the two ministers had examined the area of cultural relations and hoped for more exchanges in the cultural, scientific, and technical fields in the years to come.[10] The Soviet leaders again renewed the invitation that had already been extended to de Gaulle to visit the USSR.

On January 12, 1966, Ambassador Zorin announced to the press at the end of a meeting at the Elysée Palace that President de Gaulle would soon make an official trip to the USSR. On February 3, the press announced that his trip would take place the second week of June. The Soviet press commented that never had Franco-Soviet relations been better.

Then on April 12, shortly before de Gaulle's visit, Prime Minister Pompidou, in a speech before the National Assembly, expressed the political situation of France in these terms:

The voyage to Moscow does not represent at all what certain people would like to see in it, that is to say, some kind of reversal of alliances or threat against our European or American allies.

It is in line with our general policies favorable to the development of relations with all countries, no matter what their regime, and to a rapprochement between Eastern and Western Europe. Upon this rapprochement depends the future of peace in the world, in any case on our continent. The constant amelioration of our rapports with Soviet Russia, the happy cooperation begun between us in different realms, permits us to think that this trip will unfold itself under good auspices and contribute to a veritable détente, profitable not only to France but to all her neighbors. In progressing this way, we are eager to contribute to dissipating the climate of the cold war which has not ceased to press on the world and on Europe for twenty years.

For France, the bettering of relations with the USSR is ultimately tied to the perspective of a general détente touching the whole of international relations.[11]

Of all de Gaulle's policies, his improvement of relations with the Communist states probably met with the greatest approval in Paris. Left-wing intellectuals were willing to forget his conservative economic and social policies at home. For them, he was the author of decolonization and increased contact with Communist states. The Communist party of France was even advised not to criticize de Gaulle too much.[12]

De Gaulle's Trip to Russia

President and Mrs. de Gaulle visited the USSR between June 20 and July 1, 1966, as the guests of the Presidium of the Supreme Soviet of the USSR. Couve de Murville accompanied them throughout their trip.

At a speech delivered at a dinner given in his honor in the Kremlin the evening of his arrival, President de Gaulle said that Russia and France had been friends for many years and that there was a need to strengthen and multiply in all fields the relations between the two countries. Even though they possessed quite different regimes, like all modern nations, they were bowing to the laws of the same mechanical and scientific civilization and had more reason to understand each other. This was a polite way of saying that nations had better accommodate themselves to their diverse ideologies, since they did possess the means of annihilating each other.

He spoke of the United States and the USSR, the two super-powers which possessed diverse ideologies. Around these two superpowers, their neighbors were split into two blocs and the Cold War had spread. He indicated that France was not satisfied with the two organizations (this was an obvious reference to NATO and the Warsaw Pact) and would like to see the beginning of new relations with Eastern Europe toward détente, entente, and cooperation. Since the Soviet Union was the leading nation in Eastern Europe, de Gaulle felt it necessary to achieve this détente with the USSR first.

The alliances during the two world wars and the decisive role the USSR had played particularly in the second only strengthened Franco-Soviet solidarity. But, according to de Gaulle, the United States must also play a large role in the pacification and transformation of the world. France's primary concern in de Gaulle's eyes was the restoration of Europe to one entire whole, not the division into two diverse parts. De Gaulle ended by saying that the destiny of all Germany must be determined for the sake of the security of Europe.

During his visit, de Gaulle met with Party Secretary Brezhnev, Premier Kosygin, and the new president of the Presidium of the Supreme Soviet, Nikolai Podgorny. Couve de Murville, Andrei Gromyko, the French ambassador to the USSR, Philippe Baudet, and Ambassador Zorin participated in these meetings as well. The cordial climate permitted exchanges of views on the problems of international politics and on Franco-Soviet relations.

Primary attention was given to European problems. Both sides agreed that the first objective was détente and then the development of ties between all European countries, the independence of each, and the nonintervention into the interior affairs of each other. Both sides agreed that notable progress had been realized toward the normalization of the European situation.

The situation in Southeast Asia was examined, and it was a-greed that Vietnam was becoming more and more preoccupying because of the intensification of the war in that nation, a war that was destroying the country and making the situation in Laos and Cambodia more uncertain. Again, the French and Soviet governments stated that the only solution to the situation was a solution based on the Geneva Agreements of 1954, which meant a cease-fire, nonintervention by third parties, and supervised free elections as the means of unifying Vietnam.

De Gaulle discussed disarmament with the Soviet leaders, but no progress was made in this realm, except that both nations stressed the danger of nuclear arms. Bilateral relations between the two nations were examined. It was felt that exchanges could be increased above the objectives in the accord of October 30, 1964, which provided for a five-year commercial agreement between the two countries.

All scientific, economic, and commercial agreements then in existence were examined; and the leaders of both countries approved the creation of a Franco-Soviet commission (officially named Franco-Soviet Joint Standing Committee), composed of representatives of both countries, charged not only with examining on a regular basis problems posed by the execution of commercial, economic, and technico-scientific agreements already in existence but also with researching the possibilities of developing in these domains even wider exchanges when these present agreements ended.

The leaders of both nations decided to begin negotiations on the conclusion of a consular agreement, to pursue consultations regularly, and to establish a direct line of communication between the Kremlin and the Elysée Palace for exchanges of views and the sending of messages. De Gaulle invited Brezhnev, Kosygin, and Podgorny to visit France, and the invitation was accepted in the name of the Presidum.

De Gaulle's trip to Russia followed his successful handling of issues dividing France and her allies. He pulled French forces out of the NATO military command, removing, as he said, the danger of France's being involved in a war against her will. His move was, to a great extent, a protest against the proposal to create a multilateral nuclear force within NATO.

As far as de Gaulle was concerned, the ideological divisions of the contemporary world were less enduring than the nations of which the world is composed. He believed that the Cold War was not an ideological struggle but rather the product of a temporary bipolarity in the world.[13]

De Gaulle realized that during the nineteenth century France and Russia had stood at opposite ends of the pole. Russia had stood for absolute monarchy and territorial status quo, while France had stood for liberalism, democracy, and the reshaping of the map of Europe. In 1894, the two countries had been drawn together in an alliance by a common fear of Germany; it was an alliance between revolutionary France and reactionary Russia. Military and political interests triumphed over ideology. De Gaulle remembered the common efforts of the two countries in two world wars; but he was just as aware that the Russians would do their best to gain something from his visit without giving anything in return.[14] However, de Gaulle was a hard bargainer and the last to give something for nothing.

De Gaulle and the Soviet leaders were more in agreement on the UN, neocolonialism, and Vietnam than they were on disarmament and on European problems. De Gaulle proposed and the Soviets agreed that the United Nations should return to its initial concept, that is, to restore exclusive jurisdiction of the Security Council regarding international peace and security. This action, however, would require agreement among the Big Five in the Security Council.[15] The USSR and France refused to pay their share of the expenses for the United Nations' peace-keeping forces in Cyprus and the Congo and opposed the United States' suggestion that those nations that refused to pay their share should be deprived of their vote in the General Assembly. As discussed in an earlier chapter, de Gaulle was not particularly a fan of the United Nations. Although he recognized the necessity of the United Nations Organization and acknowledged and even encouraged its undertakings and accomplishments in the social, economic, educational, and cultural spheres, he would never agree to surrender to such an organization the right to make political decisions on behalf of his country.

The French and Soviet positions on Vietnam were similar but not identical. France wanted strict observation of the Geneva Accords of 1954, the end of all foreign intervention, the formation of a truly representative coalition government in South Vietnam, and the eventual reunification and neutralization of the country.[16] The USSR also wanted strict observation of the Geneva Accords of 1954 and the end to all foreign intervention, but in the meantime she committed herself to the National Liberation Front as the legitimate representative of South Vietnam until the reunification of the country based on free elections. De Gaulle preferred a coalition government with the NLF as participants in this government until reunification and neutralization on the basis of free elections.

But it was on Europe, the center of de Gaulle's thinking, where he and the leaders of the USSR disagreed most. Although both the USSR and de Gaulle would have liked to rid the European continent of the American presence (with some reservations), they were more in disagreement over the German problem than they were in agreement. They agreed on three basic points with regard to Germany: that the present boundaries of Germany should be recognized; that Germany (East and West) should not have nuclear weapons; that West Germany should not participate in a multilateral nuclear force in NATO.

More important, however, they disagreed on the division of Germany. The Soviet leaders never tired in their efforts to get de Gaulle to recognize East Germany and to keep Germany divided permanently. On this point, de Gaulle was at least as stubborn as any other Western leader. The Soviet leaders were so adamant on this point that it appeared as if they preferred the status quo—two military blocs face to face in Europe, the presence of 350,000 American troops on the European continent, and a divided Germany—to the alternative of the dissolution of both NATO and the Warsaw Pact, the withdrawal of all American forces, and the reunfication of Germany to the Oder and Neisse rivers. De Gaulle would no longer agree to the reunification of Germany unless she renounced the use of nuclear weapons, while the Soviet attitude was even more extreme. The USSR would only agree to the reunification of Germany under the condition that she be totally disarmed along with Eastern and Southeastern Europe. (Even under this condition, the USSR still preferred the permanent division of Germany and the recognition of two German states.) As mentioned above, de Gaulle's ultimate goal was not only the reunification of Germany but the demilitarization of all Germany and of Eastern and Southeastern Europe sometime in the future. Therefore, it appears that the long-range goals of de Gaulle and the Soviet leaders in Eastern and Southeastern Europe were similar and that their main disagreements were over the means of achieving these goals.

For the USSR, the German Federal Republic was the *bête noire*, but for France the same did not hold true. Although Franco-German relations were not what they had been in Adenauer's day, France and West Germany were held together by the Common Market, the Atlantic Alliance, and the unwillingness of the leaders of France and West Germany to see Franco-German hostility revive.

For de Gaulle, a détente did not mean the permanent division of Germany but rather the coming to terms with the nations of Eastern Europe. This was the key to his approach. He realized that this détente could only be achieved with the cooperation of the USSR; in order to discuss East European questions, he would first have to approach Moscow.[17]

Kosygin's Visit to France

Aleksei Kosygin made a trip to France in early December. He and other Soviet officials who accompanied him visited industrial enterprises and scientific and university centers. He engaged in talks with de Gaulle and Pompidou at Rambouillet that lasted several days. The general round of subjects was discussed, including European problems, disarmament, the UN, Southeast Asia, the developing nations, and economic, scientific, and technical cooperation between France and the USSR.

Both Kosygin and de Gaulle agreed that a détente was the primary step toward the evolution in relations among the European countries, regardless of their political systems. They suggested that all European countries follow the Franco-Soviet lead and develop relations in all domains. A very significant recommendation made by de Gaulle and Kosygin was the convening of a pan-European conference to examine the problems of security in Europe.

Since the visit of de Gaulle to the USSR in June, Franco-Soviet relations had progressed rapidly in the political, economic, scientific, technical, and cultural realms. De Gaulle and Kosygin examined the problems involving economic, scientific, and technical cooperation between France and the USSR, which were being worked out by a joint Franco-Soviet commission established shortly after de Gaulle's visit to Russia. The two men expressed the desire to extend their cooperation to new areas of the economy, science, and technology, and decided to establish a joint Franco-Soviet Chamber of Commerce.

The agreement to establish a Soviet consulate in France and a French consulate in Russia, which had been discussed at length during de Gaulle's visit to Russia, was signed on December 8, 1966, during Kosygin's visit to France.

Both men stressed the importance of future regular contacts between French and Soviet leaders. Premier Kosygin announced that Party Secretary Brezhnev and President Podgorny would make a visit to France sometime in the near future, and invited Prime Minister Pompidou to pay an official visit to the USSR at a time convenient to him.

The visible results of Kosygin's trip to France were meager. In spite of the warm relations that existed between France and the USSR, there still seemed to be a great contrast between de Gaulle's enthusiasm over Europe and Kosygin's restraint, at the end of 1966. They were far apart on how best to solve the problems of Europe and create the conditions necessary for a European entente. The most significant results of the trip appeared to lie in the area of impressing the Western world, primarily the United States and the German Federal Republic, as well as the Third World, at a time that many international alignments were being rethought.

The USSR was trying to use France for her own purpose while giving de Gaulle no assurances in the political realm. One Soviet correspondent from *Novosty* said: "Friendship and collaboration between our two countries will help France to implement her independent foreign policy. In her desire to free herself from the American tutelage first imposed at the time of the Marshal Plan, France needs to strengthen her ties with all countries of the world and foremost with those of Eastern Europe."[18]

The joint communiqué issued at the end of Kosygin's visit did not indicate that any of the major differences in opinion on European problems had been bridged. Even though the declaration did mention respect for the territorial integrity of all nations, this could mean one thing to France and another to the USSR, as was seen in the events of Czechoslovakia in the summer of 1968.

Franco-Soviet relations, which had been improving rapidly since the end of 1963, leveled off at the end of 1966, following Kosygin's return to Moscow, and remained in that state for more than a year afterwards.

Kosygin made a visit to Great Britain in February, 1967, and during this trip indicated that relations between Britain and the USSR had improved significantly enough to make possible the signing of a Soviet-British treaty of friendship. This suggestion by the Soviet government, although such a treaty never came to pass, irked de Gaulle, since no such gesture had been made by the Soviet government to France during Kosygin's December visit.

The British had been more active than the French at the time in exploring the possibility of negotiations on Vietnam under conditions acceptable to both sides. De Gaulle considered anything less than complete American withdrawal meaningless, and since this condition was not acceptable to the United States, it prevented him from being an effective mediator.[19] The previous summer, when de Gaulle was visiting the USSR, he had been Moscow's only important interlocutor with the West with regard to Vietnam. By February, 1967, the Soviet Union seemed to be turning to Great Britain as the mediator.

The elections of March, 1967, brought the French Communists large gains, although the Gaullists and their allies still maintained a majority in parliament. Most political analysts saw the past exchanges of visits between French and Soviet leaders as helpful to the French Communists, but the Soviet leaders did not wish to boost de Gaulle's prestige in the eyes of French Communists. Under these circumstances, the Soviet leaders decided to postpone the visit of Podgorny and Brezhnev to France at least until the fall of that year, but no definite plans were made for a visit even then.

One factor that might shed some light on the international scene was the succession to power of Kurt Kiesinger as chancellor of the German Federal Republic and Willy Brandt as foreign minister. Both men were intent upon becoming less dependent on the United States than Erhard had been, and both were looking to the East for rapprochement. With Great Britain and West Germany getting into the act, de Gaulle's policy of détente with the USSR was no longer a French monopoly.

But the most important aspect to Moscow was undoubtedly its relationship with the United States. So long as de Gaulle could influence that relationship as mediator, the USSR would cultivate his friendship, but was not willing to go to the point where Franco-Soviet friendship and cooperation would benefit France more than the Soviet Union.

Prime Minister George Pompidou's
Visit to the USSR

Prime Minister Georges Pompidou made an official visit to the USSR between July 3 and 8, accompanied by Couve de Murville. Both men spoke with Brezhnev, Kosygin, and Podgorny about the international situation and the development of Franco-Soviet relations, and agreed that over the past two or three years the friendly atmosphere that had prevailed between the two nations had led to cooperation and understanding in all fields.

The similarity between the French and Soviet positions on Vietnam had not changed. The French and Soviet leaders expressed satisfaction with the détente in Europe and again stressed that the primary goal of the détente as expressed in the Franco-Soviet Declaration of June 30, 1966, was the normalization and gradual development of relations among all European countries.

The Middle East crisis and the Six Day War between Israel and the Arab states, which had erupted the previous month, were discussed at length during Pompidou's talks with the Soviet leaders. The governments of France and the USSR expressed their regret that in the July 4, 1967 vote of the General Assembly of the UN, no decision had been reached vis-à-vis a recommendation dealing with the withdrawal of Israeli forces to the original lines they had occupied before June 5, 1967. Both governments agreed that the occupation of these territories by Israel could not be considered permanent, and expressed hope that the Security Council of the UN would work for a settlement of problems arising in that region.

It seemed as if France were taking positions on world problems identical to those of the developing countries, and thus was sounding the call of the Third World.

The leaders of both countries noted with satisfaction that the French and Soviet governments were close on some of the most important problems arising in the world today and realized the necessity of discussing them on the highest level. The leaders expressed satisfaction over Franco-Soviet cooperation in the fields of science, technology, and trade, and with the cultural and artistic exchanges. During the French prime minister's stay in the USSR, an agreement was signed between the two governments on cooperation in the cinema.

The communiqué concluded that the French prime minister's visit to the USSR and the conversations that took place on that occasion with Soviet leaders had contributed to strengthening the understanding and cooperation between the two countries and to consolidating the traditional friendship between the French and Soviet peoples.

Pompidou's visit was followed by a visit of Michel Debré, minister of economics and finances, and Maurice Schumann, minister of state in charge of scientific research, to the USSR in January, 1968. Both men met with Vladimir Kirillin, president of the State Committee for Scientific and Technical Research, and then with Premier Kosygin. Debré felt that the purchase of SECAM, the French color television process, was the most important topic discussed on his trip to Russia, because color television penetrated four important fields: commerce, technology, culture, and industry. Mr. Debré expressed satisfaction about the work performed by the Franco-Soviet Joint Standing Committee and said that the differences in structure of the two countries had not been an obstacle. Kirillin and Debré had been appointed by their respective governments and acted as co-chairmen of the committee.

Kirillin stressed that Franco-Soviet cooperation had been established for a long period and would continue far into the future, provided that no unforeseen change in circumstances occurred. The Fifth Franco-Soviet Commercial Accord, signed in 1964, had already been realized at the end of 1967. By 1969, the USSR had bought more than three and a half million francs of equipment, instead of the minimum of one million francs agreed to in the accord. Kirillin also indicated Soviet interest in increasing purchases of French equipment after the fixing of the Soviet Five Year Plan, 1970-1975.

The trip of Debré and Schumann was followed by the visit of Pierre Messmer, French minister of armed forces, to the Soviet Union in April. Messmer toured military and aircraft installations throughout the USSR. In his talks with Premier Kosygin, the two men discussed further cooperation between France and the USSR in the sphere of contacts between the armed forces of both countries.

The Events of the Spring of 1968

Domestic problems erupted into violence in France in the spring of 1968. Just when the Gaullist regime seemed at its weakest point in ten years, students who had been calm for many years in France began their manifestations against the regime, calling for a social and political overhaul. The workers joined hands with the students and struck, even though the government offered a favorable settlement both in wages and in welfare benefits. This was the most serious crisis in years, and the government barely escaped censure in parliament. De Gaulle acted quickly and firmly. He surprised many by dissolving parliament and calling for new elections. The opposition parties were caught unprepared.

De Gaulle blamed the Communists and other leftists for these demonstrations in a speech delivered on May 30, in which he also announced his decision to remain at the head of the state, while dissolving the National Assembly and holding new elections. He accused the Communists of attempting to impose a totalitarian dictatorship on France.

De Gaulle's speech on totalitarian communism brought him only slight rebuffs from the Soviet press. Although Moscow hoped for a shift to the left in the new parliamentary elections, it did not hope for a change in the president, since the USSR admired and upheld de Gaulle's foreign policy. Since the Soviet leaders considered the rapprochement with France a major factor in Soviet foreign policy, there was a fear that too much criticism of the General might cause serious repercussions in Franco-Soviet relations, if the Gaullists should win a victory in the new parliamentary elections.

The decision of the Soviet leaders not to conduct a tirade against President de Gaulle for his speech of May 30 proved to be a wise one. An apparent backlash against Communist and other left-wing demonstrators in the spring riots manifested itself in the parliamentary elections. The Gaullists and their allies won 358 out of 487 seats in parliament, while the Communists elected only 30 members, a loss of 43 seats over the election of 1967, only one year before. At the age of seventy-seven, de Gaulle was in a stronger position than he had been in at any time in the past.

Relations between France and the USSR, which had leveled off in 1967 in the political realm, began to soar again after June, 1968. Paris became the center of the international scene with the Vietnamese peace talks being held in the French capital. Even the Soviet invasion of Czechoslovakia in August, 1968, did not have long-range repercussions on Franco-Soviet relations. Although de Gaulle made it known to the Soviet leaders that the invasion of Czechoslovakia had only served to solidify the division of Europe into two camps and had acted as a setback to détente in Europe, he was equally determined not to permit this invasion to ruin his policy of building bridges to the East.

Cooperation between France and the USSR continued throughout 1968 and into 1969. Brezhnev and Podgorny did not visit France during the presidency of Charles de Gaulle, for the latter was to remain in office only until April 30, 1969. He resigned as a result of a plebiscite in which a majority of Frenchmen rejected his proposal to reduce the powers of the senate. The Soviet leaders would have most likely visited France between the Gaullist victory in the parliamentary elections of June, 1968, and de Gaulle's resignation in April, 1969, had they decided against the invasion of Czechoslovakia. Brezhnev's visit to France in October, 1971, as the guest of President Georges Pompidou would have undoubtedly come before that date had de Gaulle remained in office.

CHAPTER 7

De Gaulle's Policy toward Eastern Europe: The Period of Amelioration 1964-1969

THE evolution of relations between France and Eastern Europe during the presidency of Charles de Gaulle deserves some attention. Not much can be said about relations between France and Eastern Europe during the years 1948-1963. Although France maintained diplomatic relations with all the "socialist" countries of Eastern Europe except East Germany between the above-mentioned years, political, economic, scientific, technological, and cultural relations between France and the so-called satellite countries were held to a minimum. If de Gaulle was really sincere when he said on numerous occasions that Great Britain was an American satellite, he was well aware that this proposition held true scores of times more in speaking of the relationship between the USSR and Eastern Europe. Only when relations between France and the Soviet Union began to improve in 1964 did relations between France and Eastern Europe begin to break loose and show progress.

When de Gaulle's policy toward Eastern Europe between 1964 and 1969 is discussed, it is no surprise to find that France's relations with Yugoslavia, Poland, and Rumania were much more intimate than her relations with Czechoslovakia, Hungary, and Bulgaria. Relations between France and Albania remained practically nonexistent throughout the entire period of de Gaulle's presidency except in the diplomatic sphere.

Yugolsavia was the least orthodox of all of the "socialist" countries of Eastern Europe with regard to internal policy, and broke with the USSR in 1948. Since then, her foreign policy had been one of nonalignment.

Rumania, whose internal policy was quite orthodox from the

"socialist" point of view, began to split with the USSR on foreign policy issues in 1963, and although still theoretically a Soviet satellite and member of the Warsaw Pact, she stood apart from the other satellite nations. Culturally, she was more like France than any country of Eastern Europe. France and Rumania were the least Latin of the Latin countries, the former having been subjected to strong Germanic influences throughout the centuries, while the latter was subjected to strong slavic influences. Rumania was indeed the France of Eastern Europe, and her relationship to the Warsaw Pact and her neighbors can be compared to France's relationship to NATO and her neighbors.

Poland, whose internal policy was less orthodox than that of Rumania from the "socialist" standpoint, did not deviate from the Soviet line on foreign policy. Nevertheless, the traditional ties between France and Poland were very strong, and de Gaulle loved and admired the courage and national ardor of these people, who had for more than two centuries been the victims of German and Russian military superiority.

Ties between France and Czechoslovakia had also been strong historically. But between the Communist takeover in 1948 and the election of Alexander Dubcek as first secretary of the Central Committee of the Communist party, Czechoslovakia became and remained the most orthodox of the "socialist" countries and the most loyal to the USSR. The Dubcek interlude was too short to allow traditional Franco-Czechoslovak ties to be reborn.

Ties between France and Hungary and France and Bulgaria had historically never been close. After 1964 France's relations with these two countries showed their biggest gains in the economic, scientific, technological, and cultural areas—but not in the political realm, because of their subservience in the area of foreign policy to the USSR.

In the fall of 1965, after a visit to France by Polish Prime Minister Joseph Cyrankiewicz, de Gaulle launched a drive to improve relations with Eastern Europe. In 1966 he sent Foreign Minister Couve de Murville to visit six "socialist" countries in Eastern Europe in addition to the USSR.

In his annual New Year's address of December 31, 1966, de Gaulle said that the Cold War, which had lasted for twenty years, was in the process of disappearing, because in the East and West alike, people were growing tired of that state of permanent tension. They were becoming aware that détente, then entente, and finally cooperation among all nations of Europe would give the Continent a chance to solve its own problems. De Gaulle went on to say that France had regained her independence and would continue to direct her policies toward rapprochement in Europe by practicing fruitful and friendly relations with the USSR and by renewing close relations with Poland, Czechoslovakia, Hungary, Rumania, Bulgaria, Yugoslavia, and Albania. France would also continue to cultivate contacts with each of her neighbors and work to build the economic and, perhaps one day, political group of the Common Market nations. He closed by saying that France would help the Continent to reassemble all its states, step by step from one end to the other, so that it would become the European Europe.

Franco-Yugoslav Relations

Yugoslavia had since 1948 consistently maintained a foreign policy of nonalignment. In the course of more than twenty years, she had developed her relations above all with the Afro-Asian countries, which were the principal partners of her foreign policy. The policy of Yugoslavia had been at least as favorable to the cause of decolonization as that of the USSR.

When de Gaulle came to power in 1958, the Yugoslav government reproached him for perpetuating in Algeria a regime that was unpopular with the majority of Algerians. In 1959, Marshal Tito spoke with Ferhat Abbas, president of the Provisional Algerian Government in Belgrade, and issued a communiqué giving *de facto* recognition to this government. Two years later (September, 1961), during the plenary session of a meeting of the chiefs of state of the nonaligned nations in Belgrade, President Tito announced the *de jure* recognition of the G.P.R.A. by Yugoslavia.[1]

After the Belgrade Conference, diplomatic relations between Paris and Belgrade deteriorated rapidly. On February 2, 1962, the Quai d'orsay made it known to the Yugoslav ambassador at Paris that the French government, which had recalled its ambassador to Belgrade after Tito's recognition of the G.P.R.A., would not send a new ambassador to Belgrade. It asked the Yugoslav government to recall its ambassador to France and to reduce its diplomatic representation in Paris to that of a chargé d'affaires.

This period of tension between de Gaulle and Tito lasted only several months. The declarations of de Gaulle on the self-determination of the Algerians contributed to a rapid improvement in relations between France and Yugoslavia. The cease-fire in Algeria was hailed by President Tito with profound satisfaction, and in August, 1962, diplomatic relations between the two countries were reestablished at the ambassadorial levels. Throughout 1963, relations continued to improve with visits by French and Yugoslav delegations to each other's countries.

In June, 1964, Louis Joxe, minister of state and first member of the French government to go officially to Yugoslavia since the end of the war, signed an agreement for cultural, scientific, and technical collaboration. The French minister was received by President Tito, had talks with other Yugoslav leaders, and, at the end of his visit, made the following statement: "Franco-Yugoslav relations are developing more and more in accordance with a better mutual comprehension and affirmation of traditional ties."[2]

The visit of Mr. Joxe marked the beginning of a very close political collaboration between Belgrade and Paris. On September 16, 1964, President Tito made the following statement on French television: "I think that at the present time, France is playing a very important role. The foreign policy of General de Gaulle and of the French government has contributed in great measure to the international détente. In numerous aspects this policy can be equated to our own policy and to that of the other nonaligned countries. France is playing a very important role also inasmuch as it is a country having a long cultural tradition which, for its part, contributes to the development of humanity."[3]

The foreign policy of de Gaulle was the determining element in the promotion of Franco-Yugoslav relations after the episode over Algeria. Although the Yugoslav government did not agree with de Gaulle on the testing of nuclear weapons and on the Franco-German Treaty of 1963, the position of the French president vis-à-vis great international problems was favorably received. Tito admired de Gaulle's independence of spirit and courage of decision.

Responding to the invitation of Couve de Murville, Foreign Minister Kotcha Popovitch of Yugoslavia made an official visit to Paris in November, 1964. He met with de Gaulle, Pompidou, and Murville. At the end of the trip, the Yugoslav foreign minister commented that the meetings between Couve de Murville and himself constituted an important step toward the promotion of relations between the two countries, relations that had been developing favorably in the recent past.

Between September 11 and 14, 1966, Murville made an official visit to Yugoslavia, repaying the visit made by Foreign Minister Popovitch two years earlier. Murville was warmly received by President Tito and spoke with him about a variety of subjects. Since an agreement between France and Yugoslavia on cultural, scientific, and technological collaboration had been signed in Paris only two years before, when Louis Joxe had visited Yugoslavia, Tito's talks with Murville consisted of topics mainly in the political realm and included Europe, Germany, the Common Market, Vietnam, and bilateral relations between the two countries.[4]

One year later, in September, 1967, the new foreign minister of Yugoslavia, Marko Nikezic, was received by President de Gaulle in Paris. The two men spoke at length about the situation in the Middle East, which had erupted for the third time since 1947 only three months before, and agreed that Israel must withdraw to her borders of June 5, 1967, if there was to be peace in the Middle East. They expressed hope that the United Nations Organization would bring this conflict to an end as rapidly as possible.

In talks with Murville, the decision was made to institutionalize the contacts between ministers and high-ranking officials of both countries in the political and economic domains. The two men were in agreement vis-à-vis a détente in Europe, but not so much in agreement about the German problem.[5]

At the end of his visit on September 18, 1967, Nikezic handed de Gaulle an invitation from President Tito to pay an official visit to Yugoslavia. The invitation was accepted by President de Gaulle, but was never realized because of his resignation in April, 1969. Afterward, the Yugoslav government more than once expressed its regrets that Presidents de Gaulle and Tito never had the occasion to meet.

At the beginning of de Gaulle's presidency, the Algerian problem had considerably strained relations between France and Yugoslavia. But Algeria became independent in the summer of 1962. De Gaulle's concepts of European cooperation, his opposition to the division of Europe into two political, military, and ideological blocs, his condemnation of the war in Vietnam, his point of view of the Arab-Israeli conflict, and even his condemnation of the Soviet invasion of Czechoslovakia have been spoken of as similar and even identical to Tito's positions and ideas on these issues.

On various occasions, Marshal Tito took up the theme that his foreign policy and that of President de Gaulle were close together. On October 3, 1967, at Gospic he declared:

Our relations with France are constantly becoming better. We are tied by a long traditional friendship to France who, with President de Gaulle at its head, has given to the Western countries an example of the manner in which peace between socialist and capitalist countries can be consolidated in their reciprocal interest. De Gaulle has made a gesture of considerable importance in resisting the policies practiced by the Atlantic Pact. By his own policies he has rendered a great service to all of Europe and has reduced the dangers of a European conflict.[6]

In an interview with the *New York Times* on May 16, 1968, Tito said of de Gaulle: "I don't know how de Gaulle envisions concretely the unity of Europe, but I think like him that European security and the collaboration between European countries on the basis of equality of rights are fundamental problems. From this point of view, the interventions of de Gaulle are positive."[7]

When a representative of *Paris Match* interviewed President Tito on October 28, 1968, he asked a question with regard to the similarity between Tito's policies and those of President de Gaulle. Tito declared: "The essential fact is that our points of view on actual international problems, among them the Near East and the war in Vietnam, are almost entirely in agreement. We are in agreement on the necessity of a peaceful solution to all the international legal disputes."[8]

The series of visits exchanged in the course of the preceding years between the representatives of the French and Yugoslav governments climaxed with the trip of Mika Spiljak, president of the Federal Executive Council (prime minister) of Yugoslavia to Paris in January, 1969. At a luncheon given in Spiljak's honor shortly after his arrival, President de Gaulle lifted his glass and proposed a toast in honor of Marshal Tito, head of state of Yugoslavia. De Gaulle declared:

I would not want to miss the opportunity, Mr. President, of asking you to transmit to Marshal Broz Tito, President of the Socialist Federative Republic of Yugoslavia, my most cordial regards. The latter is addressed to the soldier, who in the worst dangers, upheld victoriously the great fight of his country. It is addressed also to the statesman whose lucid views and energetic activity reply at this very moment to that which the government of the French Republic holds as just and necessary.[9]

During Spiljak's stay in Paris, he spoke at length with Couve de Murville (then prime minister). Both men made a thorough examination of international problems and of bilateral relations between the two countries. It was established that French and Yugoslav concepts concerning the basic principles that should govern relations among all states were identical. The two countries were in agreement in affirming that progress toward peace and security implied respect for the sovereignty, independence, and equality of all states large and small, and nonintervention in their internal affairs.

The joint communiqué issued at the end of Spiljak's visit confirmed the necessity of cooperation among all states so that a climate of détente would ensue. Progress toward détente, it concluded, could only be realized if nations freed themselves from the system of blocs. Both governments stated in the communiqué that the prolongation of the Israeli occupation of Arab lands in the Middle East since the Six Day War gave rise to threats to peace. They agreed that a peaceful solution must soon be found or war would continue to break out time and time again in this area, giving rise to the threat of world conflict. The communiqué also mentioned the negotiations on Vietnam, which were progressing, and hoped for a solution to the conflict conforming to the rights of the Vietnamese people.

During Spiljak's stay in Paris an agreement was signed between France and Yugoslavia to the effect that tourist visas would no longer be required for Frenchmen and Yugoslavs visiting each other's country. An agreement on economic, industrial, and technical cooperation was signed as well.

At the end of 1968 and the beginning of 1969 it appeared as if the foreign policies of de Gaulle and Tito were so near to agreement that there was a possibility of a very close collaboration between France and the nonaligned countries. One official Yugoslav commentator speculated on the possibility of a reunion of the summit of nonaligned nations and of the necessity of enlarging the circle of participants. He was subtly referring to the possibility of nations such as France and Rumania joining the ranks of the nonaligned nations. Although de Gaulle was moving closer to the position of the nonaligned nations and wished to move away from the idea of the two power blocs, he did, nevertheless, believe that France was not only part of the West but that France needed bilateral alliances with the United States, Great Britain, and even with the German Federal Republic.

In a long declaration made on the occasion of the death of Charles de Gaulle some eighteen months after his resignation, President Tito expressed profound sorrow at the disappearance of a great and courageous figure:

Although we have not had the occasion to meet, I have nourished a sincere respect for General de Gaulle, considering him to be one without equal, a man who knew in decisive moments how to make historic decisions for France and others. De Gaulle, the soldier and statesman, consecrated his entire life to the fight for the liberty and independence of his country. Expressing my profound regret about the death of General de Gaulle, I desire to stress that I feel that his passing is not only a loss for France but also an irreplaceable loss for humanity.[10]

Franco-Rumanian Relations

France's ties with Rumania were very close between the two world wars. After 1918, Rumania, which had entered World War I on the side of the Allies, was enlarged to include Transylvania and Bukovina; the Rumanian areas of the Austro-Hungarian Empire; Dobrudja, which was ceded to Rumania by Bulgaria; and Bessarabia, which was ceded to Rumania by Russia. To maintain her post-World War I frontiers against encroachment by her former Hungarian and Bulgarian enemies, Rumania as well as Czechoslovakia and Yugoslavia maintained an alliance with France. After the dismemberment of Czechoslovakia in 1938-1939, Rumania, realizing that she could no longer rely on French protection, moved closer to the Axis powers. During World War II, Rumania was an ally of Germany and Italy; but when the war approached an end, she was occupied by Soviet troops as the Russians drove westward. Eventually, like most other countries of East-Central Europe, a Communist regime was imposed upon her.

Rumania soon became one of the most docile of the Soviet satellites, very attached to Stalinism. The internal evolution of the country was very slow. Under Party Secretary Gheorghiu Dej, democratic centralism was rigidly applied, and even during his last years in office, when the economic systems of Poland, East Germany, Czechoslovakia, Hungary, and even that of the USSR became more flexible and assigned a small place to the profit motive, Rumania remained rigid on this point. It was more difficult for Rumanians to emigrate or even travel abroad as tourists than for any of the inhabitants of other East-Central European countries.

The slowness of Rumania's internal evolution can be contrasted with her external policy, which, starting in 1963, became the most open and evolved of all the Warsaw Pact nations. Gheorghiu Dej must be credited for taking the initiative of disengaging Rumania from the Soviet line. His successors, after his death in 1965, pursued and even widened this disengagement.

Just about the time that de Gaulle began to disengage France from the foreign policy of the United States (1963), Rumania began to disengage herself from the foreign policy of the Warsaw Pact nations. The wall between France and Rumania began to crumble and the historical and intellectual ties that had united the French and Rumanian peoples traditionally were once again to manifest themselves. An identity of views on international problems, an analogous concept of international relations founded on national independence were about to reinforce traditional ties and give a new vigor to Franco-Rumanian relations. The coming together of the foreign policies of France and Rumania resulted from the fact that both countries were intent on leading a foreign policy that was national in scope as well as open and independent.

The story of the origin of Rumania's disengagement from the USSR is a most interesting one. It started in 1960 with the Soviet attempt to organize an international socialist division of labor by the specialization of tasks. Khrushchev's idea was that East Germany, Poland, Czechoslovakia, and Hungary should orient themselves toward industrial production while Rumania, Bulgaria, and Albania should devote themselves to agricultural production. The USSR felt this step necessary if the "socialist" countries were to compete with the West. Ironically, Stalinist Rumania remembered Russian history very well. She remembered that Stalin had made Russia, an underdeveloped agricultural country, into one of the two great industrial powers in the world. The Rumanian economists demonstrated that the economic specialization of "socialist" countries would end in maintaining Rumania in a situation of inferiority vis-à-vis the industrialized "socialist" nations, which were selling to Rumania goods of mediocre quality above the world market price. After Khrushchev's ouster, not much was heard about the division of labor.

Nevertheless, this plan prompted the leaders of Rumania to do much soul searching. At the end of three years, a split occurred among the Warsaw Pact nations just as in the Atlantic Pact. In 1964, Gheorghiu Dej had the Central Committee of the Communist party of Rumania adopt the following resolution:

It is the sovereign right of each socialist state to elaborate, to choose, and to change the forms and the methods of its socialist construction. No state has the right to present its own interests as general interests. Common decisions on common problems can only be made after consultation and not by the notice of a unique solution given by one sort of supranational authority. There cannot be a father party and a sons party, a superior party and a subordinate party. There exists only a big family of communist parties and workers having equal rights.[11]

On July 28, 1964, during the trip of Gheorghe Maurer, president of the Rumanian Council of State, to France, the *Manchester Guardian* wrote: "Franco-Rumanian rapprochement is the symbol of the dislocation of blocs. Mr. Maurer's trip illustrates the progressive breaking up of the two monolithic alliances of the post-war era rather than a return to old relationships which existed between France and Rumania at the time of the Little Entente."[12]

When Nicolae Ceaucescu was elected secretary-general of the Communist party of Rumania in 1965, a slow progressive liberalization continued to manifest itself. The new leaders of the party detached themselves from the Soviet line and became quite nationalistic. In all walks of life, the solidarity of the bloc was played down, and emphasis was placed on the national interests of the country. In a speech before the Central Committee of the Communist Party of Rumania, Ceaucescu declared in May, 1967: "The existence of military blocs and bases is an anachronism that is incompatible with the national independence and sovereignty of peoples."[13]

About the time of Ceaucescu's speech, Party Secretary Brezhnev made a proposal for a mechanism to coordinate the foreign policies of the Warsaw Pact nations. The Rumanian government opposed this proposal and instead suggested a reduction of Soviet control over the military institutions of the pact refusing to allow its policy to be coordinated by other nations with other policies and even put into question the usefulness of the pact itself.

During the invasion of Czechoslovakia on August 21, 1968, by five Warsaw Pact nations, Ceaucescu, in a public meeting in Bucarest, said: "There does not exist any justification, one would not be able to accept, even for a moment, any motive for permitting the idea of a military intervention into the interior affairs of a brotherly socialist state."[14] And on August 28, the Central Committee of the Communist party of Rumania issued the following statement: "The Executive Committee of the Central Committee of the Communist Party of Rumania in the name of our entire party, the entire Rumanian nation, and in the spirit of brotherly Rumanian-Czechoslovak friendship express to the communists of Czechoslovakia and to the Czech and Slovak people their sentiments of warm friendship, support and international solidarity."[15]

Moscow relied on the doctrine of limited sovereignty to justify the invasion of Czechoslovakia. According to this doctrine, a state's sovereignty is limited by its belonging to the socialist bloc. Under this doctrine the leaders of all socialist nations become collectively responsible for whatever happens in each of the socialist nations and, after consultation with other bloc nations, have the right to intervene to prevent adverse changes from coming about in a fraternal socialist country. To this thesis Ceaucescu answered to the standing jubilation of the Grand National Assembly on November 29, 1968: "The thesis they are trying to gain favor for recently, according to which the defense in common of the socialist countries against an imperialist attack supposes the limitation or renunciation of the sovereignty of a signatory state of the treaty, does not correspond to the principles of relations between socialist countries and cannot be accepted in any form."[16]

According to Ceaucescu, the Warsaw Pact could only be conceived as an organization of socialist states with equal rights. Therefore, every action and every decision undertaken in its name must be the result of the unanimous decision of all the members.

After the news of Warsaw Pact maneuvers in April, 1969, *Scinteia*, the organ of the Communist party of Rumania, condemned any military maneuver on foreign territory and said that it was necessary that European nations stop demonstrating acts of force and military maneuvers on foreign territories or near the borders of certain countries. Rumania refused to take part in these military maneuvers or allow them to take place on her territory.

During these same years (1964-1969) President de Gaulle affirmed the possibility of an independent French foreign policy and became opposed to the political and military hegemony of the two superpowers. De Gaulle's attitude was that the threat of dominance by the USSR did not justify being dominated by the United States. He was opposed to any policy, agreement, or understanding that would bring about the end of any French sovereignty whatsoever over her internal or foreign policy. Therefore, he opposed the creation within NATO of a multilateral nuclear striking force, because France would have to surrender some of her sovereignty over the decision-making process with regard to this force. He said that France's only defense was her national defense and that American troops must depart from French soil and that France must withdraw from the military aspects of NATO. Ceaucescu's policies with regard to Soviet troops and the Warsaw Pact were almost identical.

De Gaulle's policy of rapprochement dictated a necessity for good relations with countries of Central and Eastern Europe. He made it quite clear that no question of reversal of alliances was involved here, and his policy implied the end of opposing blocs.

In 1963, de Gaulle pronounced himself in favor of the neutrality of South Vietnam and against American intervention. After that, France recognized Communist China, defended the neutrality of Cambodia, condemned the UN intervention in the Congo, and the intervention of the United States in the Dominican Republic. Finally in June, 1967, de Gaulle disapproved of the policies of Israel in the Six Day War.

In the Sino-Soviet conflict, Rumania refused to choose sides. She had good relations with Communist China. She had increased her commerce with Red China starting in 1962, the year other East European countries began to decrease their trade with China. In March, 1963, she reestablished diplomatic relations with Albania. They had ceased in 1961 when the USSR and her satellites broke with Albania in retaliation for siding with Red China in the Sino-Soviet conflict. After the Six Day War in the Middle East, the other "socialist" states of Eastern Europe, including Yugoslavia, broke diplomatic relations with Israel. Rumania instead raised her representation in Israel to the ambassadorial level. Moreover, Ceaucescu's position with regard to a Middle East solution was close to that of de Gaulle: the evacuation of the territories occupied by Israel, the recognition of Israel by the Arab states, and the cessation of the state of belligerency in the Middle East.

The convergence of the foreign policies of France and Rumania led to a comparison of the roles each of the two nations played inside her respective bloc. In the Soviet camp, there was an enthusiastic approval of the independence of the French position, but one witnessed a different attitude toward the independence of Rumanian policies, which were qualified as neutralism incompatible with the obligations of a brotherly party. It was thanks to this convergence that a traditional Franco-Rumanian friendship was reborn.

A renewal of Franco-Rumanian friendship began with the visit of Gheorghe Maurer, president of the Council of State, to France in July, 1964. Because of the closeness of the international positions of France and Rumania, so many visits were made by French governmental officials to Rumania and by Rumanian governmental officials to France between 1964 and 1967 that time does not permit the author to go into detail. It is noteworthy, however, that after Maurer's visit to France in 1964, Mr. Birladeanu, vice-president of the Rumanian Council of Ministers, visited France in November, 1964, followed by the visit of Mr. Manescu, Rumanian minister of foreign affairs. In June, 1967, on returning from his trip to the UN after the Six Day War, Gheorghe Maurer stopped in Paris and had an interview with President de Gaulle. On the other side, Giscard d'Estaing in February, 1965, Couve de Murville in April, 1966, and Maurice Schumann in November, 1967, all went to Bucharest. These visits were a prelude to the visit of Charles de Gaulle to Rumania between May 14 and 18, 1968, on which he was accompanied by Couve de Murville.

President de Gaulle was the first French chief of state to make a visit to Rumania. Never in all his travels did he receive as warm a welcome from the leaders of a host country. Upon arriving at the airport in Bucharest, he was welcomed by President Ceaucescu, who exclaimed: "We appreciate highly in Rumania the position of France with regard to a whole series of essential international problems and your remarkable activity, Mr. President."[17] The importance attached to this visit so far as de

Gaulle was concerned can be seen in his failure to cancel the trip in spite of the series of domestic problems France was experiencing in May, 1968. This visit demonstrated that close ties could be established between two countries belonging to two different blocs. Here were two nations that had been united for many years by intellectual, cultural, and political ties, then separated for many years by virtue of belonging to two different blocs, and again coming together to cooperate in all realms.

Discussions between Presidents de Gaulle and Ceaucescu developed in a climate of cordiality corresponding to the sympathy that had always existed between the two countries. The two men agreed that relations founded on mutual friendship and esteem were developing satisfactorily. Since there were no problems dividing France and Rumania, rapprochement between the two countries was almost a *fait accompli*. The post-World War II period had definitely come to an end.

A reading of the joint communiqué issued on May 18 indicates that Franco-Rumanian relations were excellent in all realms including the political. It showed that the two countries were in agreement on most international problems, including European security, Vietnam, the Middle East, and the role of the United Nations Organization. As far as the economic, scientific, technological, and cultural spheres and mutual exchanges of professors, artists, scientists, and so forth, were concerned, cooperation between France and Rumania was greater than that between France and any other East European nation.

In a speech broadcast live over Rumanian radio and television, de Gaulle told the Rumanian people that he was honored, happy, and touched to visit them. He said that the French and Rumanian peoples had been friends for many years but that it had only been in the course of the great trials of this century that the full worth of Rumania was realized by France. The French were well aware that the wars, tragedies, and upheavals in the twentieth century represented sacrifices for the Rumanian people, but that the Rumanians had met these problems with full courage. After going on to say that Rumania, although reduced in size, was more Rumanian than ever, an obvious reference to Bessarabia, taken from Rumania by the USSR after World War II, he closed by praising the people for their great achievements in industry, agriculture, education, and technology.

De Gaulle then extended to President and Mrs. Ceaucescu an

official invitation to visit France. The invitation was accepted, and the date was to be set in the near future. De Gaulle was not, however, destined to meet Ceaucescu again. The latter did visit France as the official guest of President Pompidou in 1972, three years after the resignation of de Gaulle as president of France and two years after his death.

Although de Gaulle's friendship with Ceaucescu surpassed that with any other leader of a Warsaw Pact nation, and Rumania could no longer be regarded as a Soviet satellite, de Gaulle was well aware that Rumania was under Soviet pressure. Having split with the USSR in matters of foreign policy, she could not afford to stray too far from orthodox socialism in her internal policies.

Franco-Polish Relations

Franco-Polish friendship has been one of the elements that long characterized the foreign policies of the two nations. In no nation on earth (outside France) has French culture been held in higher esteem than in Poland. This was true not only between 966 and 1791, the years of independent national development for Poland, but also during the years following the partitions of Poland and again between 1919 and 1939, when Polish independence was restored.

During World War II, when Poland fell victim to German occupation, de Gaulle and the Free French recognized the Polish government-in-exile in London. In April, 1943, the USSR broke diplomatic relations with the Polish government-in-exile in London and set up the Union of Polish Patriots, composed almost entirely of Polish Communists. One year later the Union of Polish Patriots moved to Lublin, became known as the Lublin Committee, and claimed to be the provisional government of Poland. De Gaulle, Roosevelt, and Churchill refused to recognize the Lublin Committee as the legitimate representative of the Polish people since they were well aware that Polish Communists numbered no more than 3 or 4 percent of the entire nation. Only when the Lublin Committee was enlarged to include non-Communists as well, did the leaders of the Western powers agree to recognize its legitimacy as the provisional government of Poland. De Gaulle gave his recognition on June 30, 1945; the United States and Great Britain gave theirs on July 5, 1945.

Until 1948, France's relations with Poland were closer than

those with any other nation of Eastern Europe. But, with the coming of the Cold War, and strictly for artificial reasons, Franco-Polish cooperation in most realms, especially in the political realm, was ended. Catholic Poland fell victim to a Communist-dominated government that became a faithful satellite of the USSR. Only when relations between France and the USSR began to improve at the end of 1963 were Franco-Polish ties renewed.

In spite of the Franco-German Treaty of 1963, which bothered the Polish government, de Gaulle was the only Western leader who had recognized the present western frontiers of Poland as final since March, 1959. Then in July, 1964, de Gaulle gave the French position on this subject a new confirmation, when he officially declared that Franco-German views concerning the Eastern frontiers in Europe did not coincide.

Only two months after this declaration, de Gaulle sent a French parliamentary delegation to make an official visit to Poland. Since the start of the Cold War, no French or Polish governmental officials had visited each other's country. The delegation was instructed by President de Gaulle to extend an official invitation to Prime Minister Joseph Cyrankiewicz to visit France. The invitation was accepted, and Cyrankiewicz journeyed to France for an official visit.

Cyrankiewicz was the first governmental official of Poland to visit France since the war. He expressed satisfaction on the day of his arrival that de Gaulle had recognized the permanence of the present frontiers of Poland, an attitude very different from that of the leaders of France after World War I, who guaranteed France's own frontiers by means of the Locarno Pact while leaving in suspension the problem of the eastern frontier of Germany. Cyrankiewicz commended de Gaulle for his lack of silence on this subject.

Two days later, at a luncheon given in honor of Prime Minister Cyrankiewicz, de Gaulle posed the idea of an entente between France and Poland in spite of the differences in their political systems. He said: "Neither the considerations of an ideological nature nor the differences in political systems will prevent the two countries, who have been conscious for centuries of each other's worth, from remaining toward each other as they were at the depths of their being and from considering each other reciprocally."[18] Therefore, President de Gaulle proclaimed the will of France to develop her cooperation with Poland now and in the future. Thus, he proposed the limits of a Franco-Polish entente. He did not feel it indispensable for Poland to change her regime or her allies to cooperate with France actively in all domains. Nevertheless, de Gaulle realized that the possibilities for this type of cooperation would be limited at first because of the political and economic differences between the two countries.

At the end of the visit, a Franco-Polish communiqué was published. This document took note of the cordial state in which the meetings were held, meetings that had permitted a useful exchange of views on Franco-Polish bilateral relations and on the principal international problems of the times. On Vietnam, Franco-Polish points of view were similar. On the problem of normalization of relations between Eastern and Western Europe, which both agreed was an essential element in the creation of a détente, French and Polish officials deemed cooperation between the two states desirable.

As a result of Cyrankiewicz's trip to France, Valéry Giscard d'Estaing, French minister of economics and finances, journeyed to Warsaw before the end of 1965 and together with Mr. Trampczynski, minister of exterior Polish trade, signed a new commercial accord providing for a better balance of trade for Poland. The trip of Cyrankiewicz not only opened the door to an increase in cultural exchanges and cooperation in the scientific and technological areas but set the stage for regular consultations between the leaders of the two countries on foreign policy.

On May 9, 1966, a delegation of nine members of the Polish parliament made a visit to France. The fact that this delegation was headed by Zenon Kliszko, vice-president of parliament and one of the top leaders of the Polish United Workers' (Communist) Party, shows the importance the Polish government attached to this visit. Nevertheless, it was apparent from Kliszko's conversations with de Gaulle and Pompidou that Poland wanted to increase her cooperation with France mainly in the economic, not in the political, domain. In any event, even cooperation between the two countries in the nonpolitical areas was, according to de Gaulle's way of thinking, a step in the direction of détente. The trip of de Gaulle to the USSR opened the way to relations between France and the countries of Eastern Europe.

Eight months after Cyrankiewicz's visit to France and several days after that of Kliszko, de Gaulle sent Couve de Murville to

Poland to give reassurance to the Polish government concerning the ties between the two countries. During his stay, the French foreign minister signed two agreements of great importance, inaugurated a new French reading room in Cracow, and had conversations with Party Secretary Wladyslaw Gomulka, Prime Minister Joseph Cyrankiewicz, President of the Council of State Edward Ochab, and Foreign Minister Adam Rapacki.

At a dinner given in honor of Murville, his Polish counterpart, Rapacki, in a brief speech drew some positive conclusions about Murville's visit to Poland. Although Rapacki realized that there were vast differences between the economic and political systems of the two countries, he felt that friendship and entente between Poland and France would take on a constructive role.

According to the Polish leaders with whom Murville spoke, France was the only Western country capable of persuading the German Federal Republic to make certain concessions necessary for peace in Europe. But whereas the Poles were waiting for a solution to the German problem whereby the division of Germany would become permanent, de Gaulle favored the unification of Germany within the present frontiers of the two German states. While the Poles spoke of an entente between the nations of the Atlantic and Warsaw Pacts and not their decomposition, de Gaulle thought in terms of entente, which would entail a decomposition of the two blocs. Nevertheless, the Polish leaders were aware that de Gaulle was attempting to persuade the leaders of the Bonn government to modify their Eastern policies.

The meetings between Murville and the Polish leaders, numerous and deep as they may have been, were surrounded by great discretion, and no official communiqué was published. Nevertheless, the French foreign minister, in a press conference he held upon returning from Poland, expressed his satisfaction with the results of his trip, and added that he had spoken at great length with the Polish leaders about the problems of Europe that had remained in suspension since the end of World War II.

The most immediate and concrete result of the visit to Poland of Couve de Murville was the signing in Warsaw on May 20 of a cultural agreement and also one on scientific and technical cooperation. In both areas (culture on the one hand and scientific and technical cooperation on the other), a mixed Franco-Polish commission was established. Each commission coordinated its work with that of the other, and within each commission working organs were created which met periodically in Paris and Warsaw to determine what should be done in these domains between the two countries. Since French culture, which had remained strong in Poland throughout the centuries, was cut off during the period of the Cold War, these agreements gave a new pulse to the relations between the two countries. Thus the door was opened to a different climate from that which had existed during the Cold War.

The visit of Foreign Minister Adam Rapacki to France had been delayed for more than a year. He was actually supposed to have come with Prime Minister Cyrankiewicz in 1965; but, because of illness, he had not made the trip. Rapacki was renowned throughout the world, since he had presented a plan to the General Assembly of the United Nations in 1957 on the demilitarization of Central Europe. In proposing demilitarization, including East and West Germany, Poland, and Czechoslovakia, he assured the safeguarding of Polish interests and made a contribution toward détente in Europe at the same time. Rapacki saw the importance that nuclear arms were playing in the armed forces of the world powers and did not wish to allow the extension of these arms to the countries that did not already possess them.[19]

The Rapacki Plan of 1957 was unanimously opposed by the Western powers, which feared not only that Soviet forces would dominate Eastern Europe but that there would be no system of verified control of disarmament in Central Europe.

Keeping these observations of the Western powers in mind, Rapacki put forward a new plan during his visit to France which differed only slightly from the old one. According to this plan: the manufacture of all nuclear arms would be stopped at the present level; the four powers would agree not to put nuclear arms at the disposition of armies in East and West Germany, Poland, and Czechoslovakia; after goals one and two had been achieved, a complete demilitarization of this zone in Central Europe would take place; and there would be a reduction of conventional armed forces in all of Europe. This plan was enthusiastically supported by the USSR and her satellites but rejected by the Western powers. However, when the United States, the USSR, and Great Britain signed the Treaty on Non-Proliferation of Nuclear Arms in Moscow on July 1, 1968, certain objectives of the Rapacki Plan were fulfilled.[20]

Adam Rapacki received such a warm welcome from the French

government that he decided to prolong his visit an additional tw‹
days. Throughout his entire stay, he was accompanied by Murville, but on the last day of his visit he had two meetings, on‹
with Pompidou, the other with de Gaulle.

No final communiqué was issued at the end of Rapacki's visit
All that is available are an official text of the toasts offered by the
two foreign ministers during a reception at the Quai d'Orsay and
the ideas Rapacki expressed at a press conference given on
January 29 in Paris. In the toasts, Murville suggested that there
had been an encouraging evolution of Franco-Polish relations
over the past two years, while Rapacki confirmed the excellence
of these relations.

In the press conference, Rapacki expressed doubt that the
change in government in the Bonn Republic would lead to a
change in the foreign policy of West Germany, and said that
there could be no diplomatic relations between Bonn and Warsaw
until the German Federal Republic recognized the permanence
of the western frontiers of Poland, renounced the stocking of nuclear arms on its territory, and recognized the German Democratic
Republic. He also expressed the hope that a system of collective
security could be substituted for the system of opposing blocs,
but until this system came to pass, Poland would remain a faithful
member of the Warsaw Pact. On the other hand, de Gaulle felt
that, during the period of the détente, there should be a gradual
shifting away from the concept of two opposing blocs, and that
this idea of a shift should precede an entente among all European
powers that would eventually lead to a collective security agreement among all European states.

Mr. Rapacki told the reporters that during his brief stay he had
discussed economic and cultural relations between the two countries with the French leaders. He announced the opening of a
new French reading room in Warsaw, similar to the one Couve
de Murville had inaugurated at Cracow during his visit to Poland.
At the end of his stay, Rapacki reminded de Gaulle of his promise to visit Poland in the near future.

The visit of Charles de Gaulle to Poland between September 6
and 11, 1967, was the climax of Franco-Polish post-World War II
relations. All Poles were aware not only of the cultural ties that
had linked France and Poland for centuries but that de Gaulle as
a young soldier had served in Poland and that the trip he was
making to Poland was his second. In addition, the Polish genera-

ion that had resisted the German occupation in the last war had not forgotten the man who had restored confidence in his nation, which had been so shaken by the events of 1940.[21]

The reception reserved to de Gaulle by the entire Polish population exceeded in warmth and greatness even the most extravagant predictions. From the beginning of his visit, one could sense the privileged character of the friendship between France and Poland. The allocutions made by de Gaulle and the Polish leaders were underscored with a profound sincerity often absent in the empty but flowery allocutions of foreign dignitaries on official visits. The differences in the political regimes of the two countries did not seem to hinder either the conversations or the personal contacts between the leaders of both states. In the speeches given by both leaders during de Gaulle's visit, the economic and political differences of the two countries were almost always mentioned, but the reference was made to demonstrate that in spite of these differences the two countries could cooperate in all realms. The fact that France and Poland were the respective eastern and western neighbors of Germany who had suffered so much at the hands of the Germans in the last war was in itself almost enough to bind the two nations together. On numerous occasions during the visit, both de Gaulle and the Polish leaders expressed the idea that nothing bad could happen to either country that would not affect the other in an adverse manner within a short time. The fact that Poland, in the course of nearly one thousand years of existence, had never found herself at war with France was stressed with mutual satisfaction by the leaders of both countries.

From this first speech on September 6, in the course of the reception offered in his honor by Edward Ochab, president of the Polish Council of State, General de Gaulle declared: "Poles and Frenchmen, we feel that over and above the differences which the circumstances of the moment can create between us, notably with regard to our regimes, everything commands us to draw closer not only to respond to the desires of our feelings but also to support each other mutually by a cooperation as direct as possible."[22] And the president of France on this occasion put forward the idea of regular bilateral meetings in view of the principal political problems.

In response to de Gaulle, Ochab spoke of the possibility of friendship between the two countries for the progress of peace.

The fact that France and Poland belonged to two different camps served to stress the scope of such a cooperation.

On September 11, in a speech before the Polish parliament, de Gaulle said: "The fact is that the successes and the reversals of the one have always profoundly influenced the good or bad that happened to the other. . . . Despite the distance that separates them geographically, as well as diverse interior and exterior conditions that distinguish them politically, Poland and France like each other and know by instinct and experience that their destinies are linked."[23] De Gaulle went on to say that the division of Europe into two blocs was neither indispensable nor useful to the leaders of the two countries. His concept of a Europe from the Atlantic to the Urals was well received by the Polish leaders. This Europe from the Atlantic to the Urals could be more easily facilitated in de Gaulle's view because, for the first time in centuries, Poland was on good terms with Russia.

The Polish leaders were happy that de Gaulle's concept of a "Great Europe" did not regard as irreversible the breaking of the continent into two hostile blocs, and de Gaulle could not have been more elated when Wladyslaw Gomulka, in replying to de Gaulle's speech before the Polish parliament, commented: "The people of Poland pronounces itself for the liquidation of artificial barriers created by the Cold War, which have separated on our continent the Western and the Eastern countries. The social and ideological differences existing between the countries of our continent do not threaten to destroy peace."[24] Ochab also echoed de Gaulle's words when he said that the Polish government did not consider either necessary or irreversible the division of Europe into two hostile military blocs.

De Gaulle tried to visit as much of the country as possible during his brief stay in Poland. Everywhere he went, Warsaw, Cracow, Gdansk, Katowice, he was warmly received by large crowds. The very fact that he was permitted to meet and talk with students from Jagellonian University (University of Cracow), address the Polish parliament, and speak on Polish television in itself indicated the progress that had been accomplished in the relations between the two countries since the end of the Cold War.

Speaking on Polish television, de Gaulle told his Polish audience: "Peace cannot really be established in Europe except by détente, then entente, finally cooperation, practiced between all the peoples of our continent whatever might be the wounds left by their conflicts and the barriors built up by their regimes."[25]

It was impossible for anyone to expect that this trip would bring about radical changes, such as an alliance between Poland and France; but this visit, which would have been impossible to imagine even a few years earlier, revealed a new spirit in Europe.

The leaders of the two nations had stated on several occasions over the previous two years that relations between France and Poland were developing and intensifying themselves. But the conversations de Gaulle had with the Polish leaders did not relate exclusively to Franco-Polish problems. In the course of these meetings, they proceeded to a large exchange of views on the principal problems touching world politics. The détente in Europe, the war in Vietnam, the Middle East situation, and the German problem all were discussed. De Gaulle and the Polish leaders were almost in total agreement vis-à-vis the settlement of the Middle East and Vietnam problems.

As far as Vietnam was concerned, the two governments condemned even the basis of this war. They desired to return to the Geneva Accords of 1954 and asked that the right of the Vietnamese people to settle their own affairs be safeguarded.[26] On the Middle East, it was agreed that Israel must withdraw to her borders of before the Six Day War. On Germany, they disagreed as to whether there should be one or two German states, but with regard to the boundaries of Poland, there was no disagreement.

It was the problem of détente, however, that received the most attention in their discussions. The possibility of the opening of a conference on European security was envisaged. De Gaulle and the Polish leaders felt that cooperation between France and Poland should serve the cause of a European détente precisely because of their ideological differences.

Finally, de Gaulle and the Polish leaders stressed with satisfaction that this visit had demonstrated the vitality of Franco-Polish friendship and decided to continue the regular consultations on questions of interest to Poland and France. Before his departure, de Gaulle invited Gomulka, Cyrankiewicz, and Ochab to make an official visit to France. The invitation was accepted, and the date was to be fixed in the near future.

Franco-Polish relations in all realms continued to move ahead after de Gaulle's return from Poland. Among the attributes stemming from the visit to Poland, an important place must be assigned to the meetings of diplomats organized for the purpose of discussing the problems of interest to the two countries.

Between February 4 and 7, 1968, Polish Vice-Minister of Foreign Affairs Winiewicz journeyed to France and had meetings with Couve de Murville. Mr. Marcellin, French Minister of Groundwork, made a visit to Poland between March 1 and 3, 1968, and the following month Polish Minister of Foreign Commerce Trampczynski went to France to discuss the modes of application of the last Franco-Polish agreements. In the course of all of these visits some meetings were held in Warsaw between May 27 and 29 on the extension of Franco-Polish industrial cooperation, considered indispensable to remedy the deficit in the commercial balance of payments.

With the invasion of Czechoslovakia by five Warsaw Pact nations including Poland on August 21, 1968, Franco-Polish relations came to a halt for a short time. On August 26, 1968, the Polish Ambassador to France was called to the Quai d'Orsay by Couve de Murville to give an explanation of the attitude of the Polish government vis-à-vis these most recent developments. Gomulka's visit to France was deferred. However, in spite of the invasion of Czechoslovakia, cooperation between de Gaulle and the Polish leaders, which had been started several years before and by then was well established, was taken up again within several months, when numerous French and Polish delegations in all realms visited each other's country.

As with Brezhnev's visit to France, the visit of Gomulka to Poland would have come to pass if de Gaulle had not resigned in April, 1969. In addition, Gomulka and Cyrankiewicz were replaced in the fall of 1970 as a result of internal stresses and strains. Eventually President Pompidou offered the invitation to the new Polish leaders, and between October 2 and 6, 1972, Party Secretary Edward Gierek made an official visit to France.

Franco-Czechoslovak Relations

Czechoslovakia, like Poland, was traditionally an ally of France, but historically did not enjoy so long a period of independent development as did Poland. Whereas Poland was an independent nation at least between 966 and 1791, Czechoslovakia did not enjoy a long period of independent development before World War I. As a result of the defeat of the Austro-Hungarian Empire in World War I, she was broken up, and the various nationalities were given the right to form states of their own. The new state of Czechoslovakia was created by merging Bohemia, Moravia, and Slovakia as well as Ruthenia, which had all lived under Habsburg rule prior to 1918. From 1918 until the dismemberment of Czechoslovakia in 1938, Franco-Czechoslovak relations were so close that Czechoslovakia has sometimes been spoken of as a French satellite (by choice) during those years. After World War II, Franco-Czechoslovak relations were again close until the Communist takeover in 1948. When Franco-Soviet relations began to improve in 1964, de Gaulle hoped that France's relations with Czechoslovakia could again become closer.

Couve de Murville was sent on an official visit to Czechoslovakia on behalf of President de Gaulle between July 25 and 28, 1966. He spoke with President Novotny, Prime Minister Jozef Lenart, and Foreign Minister Vaclav David. At the end of his visit, he stated that France and Czechoslovakia had been friends for a long time and particularly during the last forty or fifty years many ties had been established between the two peoples. Murville felt that time had passed and circumstances were different. It was time to renew the relations that had formerly existed between the two countries and that had been from every standpoint very close.

Between October 23 and 26, 1967, Jozef Lenart and Vaclav David paid an official visit to France, spoke at length with Pompidou and Couve de Murville, and were also received by President de Gaulle. The talks permitted a useful exchange of views on the problems of international politics as well as on Franco-Czechoslovak relations. Both sides agreed that there was an upward trend in the development of relations between East and West on the European continent not only in the political realm but on the economic, cultural, scientific, and technical levels as well. This improvement in East-West relations should serve as the basis for examining major political problems facing Europe, including the German problem and European security.

Both sides expressed concern about the escalation of the war in Vietnam and were in agreement that only an end to external intervention and a return to the Geneva Accords of 1954 would contribute to putting an end to the conflict.[27] On the Middle

East, the French and Czechoslovak leaders were in agreement that Israel must withdraw to her borders that existed before June 5, 1967, and hoped that the United Nations Organization would soon find a solution to the problem.

Economic, scientific, and technical relations between the two countries had developed sufficiently well since the signing of a long-term agreement in Prague in October, 1965, and there had been an encouraging rise in the volume of trade between the two countries. The program of exchanges of scientists, professors, and technicians, which was also signed in October, 1965, had already gone into effect in 1966 and seemed to be working well.

A cultural agreement was signed between Couve de Murville and Vaclav David on behalf of their countries on the last day of the visit of Lenart and David to France, and provided means by which the French and Czechoslovak people could acquire a better understanding of each other's civilization and language.[28] Later Prime Minister Lenart invited Premier Pompidou to pay an official visit to Czechoslovakia. The invitation was gladly accepted, but no date was set for the visit.

Pompidou was not destined to visit Czechoslovakia because of circumstances unforeseen at the time of Jozef Lenart's visit to France. Aside from Pompidou's replacement as premier by Couve de Murville at the end of June, 1968, there were the rapid shifts in the leadership of Czechoslovakia and the tragic events the year 1968 brought to that unfortunate country.

After twenty years of hard-core Communist rule, a more liberal communism began to manifest itself within the Central Committee of the Communist party of Czechoslovakia. Antonin Novotny, a Stalinist Communist who had managed to survive the purges of the Thaw to which most of his colleagues in other East European countries fell victim, was finally forced to resign as first secretary of the Czechoslovak Communist party on January 4, 1968. Two days later, Alexander Dubcek, a more progressive Communist, was elected to fill the post of party secretary. In Czechoslovakia, it was understood that neither the Czechs nor the Slovaks should hold both the positions of party secretary and prime minister, the two most important posts. Since Jozef Lenart, like Dubcek, was also a Slovak, there was pressure upon him to resign as prime minister and make way for a Czech. But pressure to resign was put on Lenart for a different reason as well. Lenart, like Novotny, was identified with the old-guard, more conservative type of communism not in vogue with the majority of the Central Committee at the time. Lenart's resignation as prime minister and his replacement by Oldrich Cernik killed two birds with one stone. Cernik was not only a Czech but a progressive Communist as well. Novotny, who had held the posts of party secretary and president simultaneously, resigned as president of Czechoslovakia on March 28, and General Ludwik Swoboda, a veteran Communist, was chosen in his place. By April, there had been a complete change in leadership at the top.

Because of the inability of these new leaders to reconcile their differences with the old-guard rulers of the USSR, Czechoslovakia was invaded in the late evening of August 20 and early morning of August 21, 1968, by Soviet, Polish, East German, Hungarian, and Bulgarian troops. Immediately, the Security Council of the UN reconvened, and opened its debate on the evening of August 21. U Thant, Secretary-General of the UN, launched an appeal to the Soviet Union to withdraw. The Security Council passed a resolution presented by seven Western nations, condemning the Soviet invasion of Czechoslovakia and demanding the withdrawal of all foreign troops from Czechoslovakia by a ten to two margin with three abstentions.[29]

President de Gaulle received Czechoslovak Ambassador Pithart on August 22 and was in total agreement with the ambassador in demanding the unconditional release of the top Czechoslovak leaders arrested by Soviet Troops on August 21 and the withdrawal of all foreign troops from Czechoslovakia.[30] Throughout the entire incident, de Gaulle made it clear that he was 100 percent behind the Czechoslovak leaders in their struggle against Soviet hegemony.

Finally on August 24 the Czechoslovak leaders were released and allowed to take part in negotiations with the Soviet leaders in Moscow. A compromise was reached between the Soviet and Czechoslovak delegations on August 27, and the Czechoslovak representatives at the United Nations asked to remove the Czechoslovak question from the agenda of the Security Council. The agreement provided that the present leaders of Czechoslovakia would be permitted to remain in power while allowing Moscow to call the shots. East European troops would leave the country while Soviet troops would remain. Eventually, most of the Soviet troops would be withdrawn, but some would stay indefinitely. It was apparent that the USSR had won the day. With

Soviet troops in Czechoslovakia indefinitely, Russia could assure the removal of those leaders in positions of power, and replace them with hard-core Communists while retaining in office a few independent-minded Communists like President Ludwik Swoboda, whose post was ceremonial.

Franco-Czechoslovak political relations remained static between the invasion of Czechoslovakia in August, 1968, and April, 1969, the month de Gaulle resigned as president of France and Dubcek was ousted as party secretary and replaced by the moderate communist Gustav Husak. Nevertheless, economic, cultural, scientific, and technological relations between the two countries continued to improve at a rapid pace.

Franco-Hungarian Relations

Traditionally, there had never existed between France and Hungary the close relationship that existed between France and Czechoslovakia. But in 1964, when relations between France and the Soviet Union began to improve, Foreign Minister Janos Peter of Hungary made an official visit to France. Between Peter's visit to France in 1964 and Couve de Murville's to Hungary in 1966, various members of the French and Hungarian governments paid visits to each other's country.

During Couve de Murville's visit to Hungary, between July 28 and 30, 1966, he found in that nation much esteem and respect for France, her government and policy, and a desire to establish close economic and cultural ties with France. Murville's trip to Hungary served a double purpose: it was a gesture of de Gaulle's policy of good will toward Hungary, as well as a repayment for the visit Peter paid to de Gaulle in 1964, when relations between the two countries were just beginning to undergo an improvement. Although Murville's visit to Hungary was relatively short, it set the stage for the development of relations between France and Hungary. Both governments agreed that there were no conflicts of interest and no disputes between the two countries, while both shared close viewpoints on many problems of international policy and on the future of Europe. At the end of the visit, Couve de Murville invited Hungarian Prime Minister Jeno Fock and Foreign Minister Janos Peter to visit France at a time convenient to them.

The French offer was taken up between March 25 and 30,

1968, when Fock, Peter, and Deputy Minister of Foreign Trade Darvas made an official visit to France. These men had extensive talks with Pompidou and Couve de Murville and were cordially received by President de Gaulle. European problems were given first preference in the list of topics discussed. Both governments agreed on the necessity of developing relations between European countries in all domains including the political realm.[31] On Vietnam, both governments agreed that the return to the Geneva Accords of 1954 and an end to all foreign intervention would make it possible to terminate the conflict and to guarantee to the Vietnamese people the possibility of determining their destiny.[32]

Both governments noted with satisfaction the evolution of economic relations between the two countries over the years. France and Hungary agreed to establish a joint commission with the view of encouraging their cooperation in industrial, technological, and scientific matters.[33] The French and Hungarian leaders agreed that cultural relations between the two countries were developing well in accordance with the cultural agreement signed between the two countries on July 28, 1966, during Murville's visit to Hungary. The agreement provided for an increase and diversification of contacts between French and Hungarian writers, artists, teachers, and scientists in order to facilitate a better knowledge of respective civilizations and languages.

At the end of the visit, Prime Minister Fock, on behalf of the Presidential Council and the Council of Ministers, invited President de Gaulle and Prime Minister Pompidou to make an official visit to Hungary. Although both men gladly accepted, Pompidou only remained prime minister three additional months and de Gaulle, president for one additional year. Neither the time nor the occasion arose for either man in his official capacity to make a visit to either Hungary or Czechoslovakia.

Franco-Bulgarian Relations

As with Hungary, relations between France and Bulgaria were not traditionally close. When relations began to improve between France and the USSR in 1964, the Bulgarian government sent Foreign Minister Ivan Bazhev to Paris on an official visit.

In comparison to the other countries of East-Central Europe, it appears that France's relations with Bulgaria were the least developed in 1964-1965, with the exception of Albania, a Chinese satellite. De Gaulle was anxious to increase relations with Bulgaria in all spheres. Therefore, Couve de Murville was sent on an official visit to Bulgaria between April 28 and 30, 1966, before his visits to Czechoslovakia and Hungary in July. The Bulgarians expressed a desire to purchase more French capital goods during Couve de Murville's visit. Up until this time, French trade with Bulgaria had been restricted in accordance with the exports of Bulgarian goods (primarily agricultural products, and especially tobacco) to France. Murville believed that his trip to Bulgaria helped to strengthen France's ties with that country. On behalf of President de Gaulle, he invited Todor Zhivkov, president of the Bulgarian Council of Ministers (prime minister), to visit France.

Between October 10 and 15, 1966, Zhivkov, accompanied by Foreign Minister Bazhev and Ivan Popov, chairman of the State Committee on Science and Technical Progress, paid an official visit to France in accordance with de Gaulle's invitation. The fact that Popov accompanied the prime minister and foreign minister indicates that the Bulgarian government was anxious to increase scientific and technological progress with France.

During the October visit, de Gaulle received Zhivkov. The latter, joined by Bazhev and Popov, engaged in extensive talks with Pompidou and Murville. These conversations permitted a thorough exchange of views on major international problems and on the favorable development of relations between France and Bulgaria in recent months.

Unlike the talks with Czechoslovakia and Hungary which would take place later, where time was divided almost equally between political problems in Europe and the world on the one hand, and economic, scientific, technological, and cultural exchanges on the other, talks between France and Bulgaria dealt almost entirely with the latter. After a brief mention of European questions and détente, and agreement between Bulgaria and France on Vietnam, the leaders of both countries went on to discuss economic relations between the two countries. The Bulgarian prime minister said that his country would buy mostly capital goods from France. The French leaders agreed to study the idea of increasing purchases from Bulgaria to create a better balance of trade between the two countries. Still, trade between France and Bulgaria was far less than that between France and the other nations of East-Central Europe.

A long-term Franco-Bulgarian cultural agreement was signed by the two countries, particularly in the areas of universities, art, and cinematography as well as book sales and exchanges of tourists and young people. The two governments agreed to develop reciprocal teaching of their languages.[34] The Scientific and Technical Cooperation Agreement, signed the same day, expressed the intention to encourage Franco-Bulgarian collaboration and exchanges in the area of basic research, the peaceful uses of atomic energy, and industrial research. It would help to facilitate the relations both countries wished to develop between their scientists, researchers, and technicians. An agricultural arrangement was also concluded within the general framework of scientific and technical cooperation.[35]

At the end of the visit, Prime Minister Zhivkov invited President de Gaulle and Prime Minister Pompidou to make an official visit to Bulgaria at a convenient date. These visits, like those to Czechoslovakia and Hungary, never came to pass for reasons mentioned above.

One additional agreement was signed between France and Bulgaria when Maurice Schumann, minister of state for scientific and technical research, visited Bulgaria in December, 1967. Schumann and Mr. Popov, president of the Bulgarian Committee for Science and Technology, signed an agreement calling for cooperation between the French Atomic Energy Commission and the Bulgarian Committee for Peaceful Use of Atomic Energy.

It can readily be seen that because of the status of Czechoslovakia, Hungary, and Bulgaria as satellites of the USSR, de Gaulle's relations with these nations from 1964 to 1969 were confined mainly to the economic, scientific, technological, and cultural areas, not to the political realm. Yet de Gaulle made as great an effort as possible toward accommodation and détente in Eastern Europe, given the circumstances of these nations.

De Gaulle realized that the restored friendship between France and Eastern Europe had to take into account some political realities that people in both blocs would like to see changed. The USSR watched over the cohesion of the Communist camp. It had strategic interests in Central and Eastern Europe. But de Gaulle would not permit the Czechoslovak affair to end a détente between, East and West. His policy toward the East rested on the conviction that in the end, the evolution of the "socialist" states was inevitable. Under these circumstances, it was necessary to refrain from the exploitation of episodes such as Czechoslovakia, so that the world could avoid returning to the politics of the confrontation of blocs.

CHAPTER 8

Summary and Conclusion

W HY did de Gaulle propose a referendum on a very controversial issue on April 27, 1969, and stake his political future on the outcome of this referendum? The question becomes even more perplexing when one takes into account that only eleven months before the referendum, de Gaulle and his followers had won the greatest political landslide in the parliamentary elections since the founding of the Fifth Republic.

In this referendum, de Gaulle not only proposed that the powers of the senate be drastically reduced but that the central government be divested of many of its powers in the areas of economic planning, investments, urban development, and regional development. He proposed to give these powers to the new regional units, which were a little larger than the old departments. It seemed as if public opinion was against reducing the powers of the senate and in favor of granting additional powers to the regional units. But de Gaulle refused to allow the people to vote on these two issues separately and submitted them for a vote as a package deal.

The Communists and Socialists who traditionally favored the abolition of the senate altogether voted yes, but the Gaullists were split down the middle. The final vote was 53.18 percent no and 46.81 percent yes. De Gaulle lost the referendum and immediately resigned as president of France.

Perhaps de Gaulle was pushing the odds and hoped that he would lose so that he could use this as a pretext to retire. The General was then seventy-eight years of age and ailing. One could notice a marked deterioration in his physical appearance during his last two years in office. Hindsight has demonstrated that even if he had won the referendum, he would not have lived to finish out his term in office, which was due to expire in 1972.

No statesman of the twentieth century has to this date been

more consistent in his policies than Charles de Gaulle. He believed above anything else that nationalism is the most unifying of all forces. His entire foreign policy was, moreover, attuned to this belief.

When he told the Rumanian people on May 18, 1968, while on an official visit to their country, that Rumania, although reduced in size, was more Rumanian than ever, he was expressing more than his sympathy for the Rumanians in their loss of Bessarabia to the USSR after World War II. He was also telling them that as a result of this loss, Rumania was more ethnically Rumanian and thus stronger and more united.

On several occasions, de Gaulle made reference to Poland's loss of her eastern territories to the USSR after World War II, most of which were Ukrainian and White Russian. As a result of these losses, de Gaulle felt that Poland, although reduced in size, was internally stronger than she had been prior to World War II, when she had had to cope with numerous ethnic minorities. Only 66 percent of all people living in Poland between the two world wars were ethnic Poles, whereas, after the loss of the eastern territories, 99 percent of all people living in Poland were Polish; and the frontiers, although reduced in size, were much more defendable.[1]

De Gaulle understood the aspirations of the peoples of the developing nations who were struggling for their national identity. He was loved and respected in the Third World, where he so often stood up for the developing countries and opposed the designs of the "Western Imperialists," thereby lining up with the Communist bloc countries against his own allies. Then in 1967, when the Ibos of Nigeria began to wage a war of independence against the Nigerian government and set up a new state known as Biafra, de Gaulle was sympathetic to the cause of the Ibos. Most of the developing nations backed Nigeria in this struggle, while de Gaulle supported the secessionist movement of the Ibos and in 1968 agreed to recognize the state of Biafra. This time, the United States and Great Britain sided with the Communist bloc countries and most of the developing nations in their support for Nigeria. But de Gaulle was consistent in his policies. The Christian Ibos were of a different nationality (tribe) from the two other principal tribes of Nigeria (Yoruda and Hausa), who were of the Islam faith, and de Gaulle felt that the Ibos should have a nation-state of their own.

To what extent did Charles de Gaulle succeed in achieving his "Grand Design" of building one Europe from the Atlantic to the Urals? To give a simple answer, one cay say that Europe still remains divided into two parts. But if we search through all de Gaulle's speeches, announcements, and press conferences in which he makes references to one Europe from the Atlantic to the Urals, he states either explicitly or by implication that his "Grand Design" will not be accomplished in a short time, and never within his lifetime. The importance of de Gaulle's contribution to the world is that he set in motion his "Grand Design," which could well lead to the establishment of one Europe.

In the last paragraph of the preface to this work, I stated that although many people feel that Europe from the Atlantic to the Urals is a utopian ideal, it is their misunderstanding of de Gaulle's "Grand Design" that leads them to this conclusion. This misunderstanding lies in their belief that de Gaulle wanted to build one supranational Europe from the Atlantic to the Urals, while in fact no individual could have been more opposed to a supranational Europe than the political realist de Gaulle himself. De Gaulle was adamant in his belief that only the government of each nation has the right to make decisions on behalf of its people and that the people of each nation would never agree to submit to the decisions of a supranational authority.

De Gaulle's "Grand Design" was to build one Europe from the Atlantic to the Urals, a loose confederation of European states with each retaining full sovereignty. Each European state would cooperate with every other in the cultural, social, economic, and political realms. Organs would be set up to coordinate the activities of all European states in the above-mentioned areas, and eventually these states would arrive at common policies. This cooperation among all European states would only be achieved after a détente and entente had ensued between the states of Eastern and Western Europe.

Détente and entente had already been achieved between the nations of Western Europe by 1949; and soon after, these nations started an intensive program of mutual cooperation not only in the fields of culture, science, and technology but in the field of economics as well. In the 1950's, organizations such as EURATOM, the European Coal and Steel Community (ECSC), and the European Economic Community (EEC) were created by six nations of Western Europe to coordinate their atomic energy, coal and steel, and economic programs. In 1965, the European Six signed a treaty to fuse the institutions of the EEC, EURATOM, and the ECSC.

Cooperation in the political realm proved to be slow, however. Therefore, in the early 1960's, Charles de Gaulle, before seriously undertaking a policy of détente with the USSR and East-Central Europe, presented a plan calling for a very loose confederation between the European Six, a union of sovereign states. He suggested that the Six form a political, defense, and cultural commission to coordinate their activities in these three fields. De Gaulle was seeking to achieve a common foreign and defense policy for the European Six. He felt that if the other five were to accept his plan, other nations in Western Europe would soon join the Six and a loose political union would be achieved among the nations of Western Europe. The Benelux countries were the most opposed to this plan, since they felt it did not go far enough and held out for nothing less than a supranational Western Europe. De Gaulle's plan fell through, but he did not give up. In January, 1963, France signed a treaty of mutual cooperation with the Federal Republic of Germany that attempted to put into effect de Gaulle's plan for political, defense, and cultural cooperation between the two, since he had not succeeded in achieving it with the Six. This treaty did not prove to be as fruitful as either de Gaulle or the leaders of the GFR had hoped because of the vast differences in the defense and foreign policies of the two nations. But de Gaulle did not give up that easily. He felt assured that in time the nations of Western Europe would realize the impossibility of a supranational Western Europe and accept his more realistic plan for a loose confederation.

De Gaulle continued to propagate his plan for the political unification of Western Europe, even though the Franco-German Treaty of Mutual Cooperation proved to be something of a disappointment. At the same time, he began an intensive program of seeking a détente with the Communist nations of Eastern Europe that had been traditional allies of France. While increasing France's cooperation with the "socialist" states in the economic, scientific, technological, and cultural spheres and seeking a common policy between France and these countries vis-à-vis problems in Europe, Vietnam, the UN, and the developing nations, he embarked on a policy of trying to free Europe from the concept of two hostile blocs, one dominated by the United States

and the other by the USSR. During the period of détente between East and West in which France would assume the lead, de
Gaulle would withdraw his country from NATO and embark upon
a foreign policy of independence while remaining loyal to the Atlantic Alliance.

Rumania was acting in a similar manner with regard to the
Warsaw Pact. De Gaulle hoped that other nations in Eastern and
Western Europe would follow the leads of France and Rumania,
but during the period of détente, he believed that it was still
premature to completely dissolve the Atlantic Alliance and the
Warsaw Pact. Therefore, détente would consist of a mutual understanding between the nations of Eastern and Western Europe
and a more independent foreign policy on the part of all European states. During the era of détente, the defenses of each
European state would acquire a more national character. De
Gaulle believed that a number of years would pass before even
the détente could be achieved.

During the very final stages of the détente, de Gaulle envisaged a Europe in which both the Atlantic Alliance and the Warsaw Pact could be dissolved, although France would remain in alliance with the United States and Great Britain. Perhaps some of
the nations of Eastern Europe would voluntarily remain in alliance with the USSR, but by this time, they would have acquired a great degree of independence in their foreign policies.
The two German states would be reunited as far as the Oder and
Neisse rivers and would, if given a free choice, be capitalist or at
most social democratic. De Gaulle felt that the USSR would
agree to the reunification of Germany after the period of the
détente, provided that Germany as well as Eastern and Southeastern Europe became a demilitarized zone. All remaining
American troops would withdraw from Western Europe. Whereas
"socialist" Eastern Europe would continue to look to the USSR
for political leadership, Western Europe would look to France,
the strongest power in continental Western Europe, for its political guidance. De Gaulle felt that by this time at the latest, the
political unification of Western Europe would be a reality.

During the period of the entente, a treaty of mutual security
would be signed by the United States, Canada, and all nations of
Europe from the Atlantic to the Urals. After the entente, the nations of Eastern and Western Europe would undertake a program
of cooperation first in the economic realm, where they would

build organs comparable to those of the EEC, and then in the political realm, until one Europe would be created; it would be a political union of all nations of Europe (loose confederation), with each maintaining its sovereignty.

In his press conference of September 9, 1968, after again condemning the Soviet invasion of Czechoslovakia, de Gaulle explained why he believed his Europe would ultimately become a reality in the following words:

It is indeed too late for foreign domination to win the support of nations anywhere, even when it has conquered their territory. As for converting them, it is too late for any ideology, notably communism, to prevail over national sentiment. In view of the general aspiration toward progress and peace it is too late to succeed in dividing Europe forever into two opposed blocs. That is to say that France, while endowing herself with the means necessary to remain herself and survive, come what may, will continue to work everywhere, and first in our continent, on the one hand for the independence of peoples and the freedom of men, on the other, for détente, entente and cooperation, in other words for peace.[2]

De Gaulle was convinced that nationalism would force the evolution of communism in Eastern Europe to the point where these nations would be ready to cooperate with Western Europe.

De Gaulle believed that Europe ended at the Urals. Beyond this range of mountains lie Soviet colonies, territories that could one day be disputed by Communist China or other nations seeking their independence from Russia, just as the developing nations of Asia and Africa sought their independence from the "Western Imperialists" after World War II. Russia, which is culturally part of Europe, would ultimately be forced to turn to Europe economically, politically, and militarily.

The initial stages of détente in Europe have already come to pass. The German Federal Republic, under the leadership of Willy Brandt, has not only agreed to recognize as final the loss of former German territory east of the Oder and Neisse rivers to Poland but has also agreed to exchange diplomatic representatives with the German Democratic Republic. The German Federal Republic will have established diplomatic relations with all of the "socialist" countries of Eastern Europe by the end of 1974, with the possible exception of Albania. President Georges Pompidou of France has already extended diplomatic recognition to the German Democratic Republic, and the United States and Great Britain have agreed to recognize East Germany before the end of 1974. If German unity eventually becomes a reality, the initial steps will have to be taken by the two German states themselves. In any event, if German reunification eventually emerges, it will occur somewhat further in the future than de Gaulle had anticipated.

Considerable progress has been made in the last few years in the direction of détente. It is still too early to tell whether or not the Europe de Gaulle envisaged will eventually emerge, but one can say with certainty that the Europe that eventually does emerge will be one in which France will play a major role. De Gaulle's dream will not have been in vain.

Notes and References

Chapter 1

1. *Lettres de M. Guizot à sa famille et à ses amis*, ed. Mme de Witt née Guizot (Paris, 1884), pp. 270-271, taken from Jean-Baptiste Duroselle, "Changes in French Foreign Policy Since 1945," *In Search of France* (Cambridge: Center for International Affairs, Harvard University, 1963), pp. 307-308.
2. Alexander Werth, *De Gaulle* (Middlesex, England: Penguin Books Ltd., 1967), p. 57.
3. *Ibid.*, p. 59.
4. *Ibid.*, p. 55.
5. Stanley Clark, *The Man Who Is France* (New York: Dodd, Mead and Company, 1960), p. 73.
6. *Ibid.*, p. 21.
7. Werth, *op. cit.*, p. 74.
8. *Ibid.*, p. 75.
9. Clark *op. cit.*, p. 73.
10. De Gaulle, *Mémoires*, I, 22.
11. *Ibid.*, 83-84.
12. Jean Lacouture, *De Gaulle* (New York: The New American Library, 1965), p. 80.
13. *Ibid.*, p. 81.
14. Milton Viorst, *Hostile Allies: FDR and De Gaulle* (New York: Macmillan Company, 1965), p. 47.
15. *Ibid.*, p. 146
16. *Ibid.*, p. 150.
17. Edgar S. Furniss, Jr., *France: Troubled Ally* (New York: Council on Foreign Relations, 1960), pp. 5-6.
18. *Ibid.*, p. 16.

Chapter 2

1. Robert G. Neumann, *European Government*, 4th ed. (New York: McGraw-Hill Book Co., 1968), pp. 288-289.
2. *Ibid.*, p. 290.

3. *Major Addresses, Statements and Press Conferences of General Charles de Gaulle, May 19, 1958-January 31, 1964* (New York: French Embassy), p. 12.
4. *French Affairs*, No. 84 (New York: French Embassy, May, 1959), p. 7.
5. *Ibid.*, p. 8.
6. When the franc was devalued in 1958, a currency reform was put into effect as well. Thus, one hundred old francs equaled one new franc.
7. *French Affairs*, No. 84, p. 9.
8. *Major Addresses . . . of General Charles de Gaulle, op. cit.*, p. 159.
9. *Ibid.*, pp. 54-55.
10. Werth, *De Gaulle*, p. 258.
11. *Major Addresses . . . of General Charles de Gaulle, op. cit.*, p. 73.
12. *Ibid.*, p. 88.
13. Werth, *op. cit.*, p. 275.

Chapter 3

1. In the summer of 1958, the king of Iraq was assassinated and a left-wing coup replaced the pro-Western government. The same rebels threatened to assassinate the king of Jordan, while pro-Nasser elements vowed to overthrow the pro-Western government of Lebanon. President Eisenhower immediately sent the American marines to Lebanon and Macmillan sent the British navy to Jordan to check Soviet and Egyptian operations in the area.
   Quemoy and Matsu are two islands off the coast of mainland China that were being shelled daily by the Chinese Communists. President Eisenhower said his administration would defend these islands in case of an attempted Chinese invasion.
2. John Newhouse, *De Gaulle and the Anglo-Saxons* (New York: The Viking Press, 1970), p. 87.
3. *Major Addresses . . . of General Charles de Gaulle, May 19, 1958-January 31, 1964*, p. 49.
4. Newhouse, *op cit.*, p. 37.
5. *Major Addresses . . . of General Charles de Gaulle, op. cit.*, p. 61.
6. *Speeches and Press Conferences*, No. 147 (New York: French Embassy, December 30, 1959), p. 7.
7. *Ibid.*
8. The Common Market, which is officially known as the European Economic Community, was created in 1957 by the Treaty of Rome. It included six members originally: France, West Germany, Italy, Belgium, the Netherlands, and Luxembourg. These same six also belonged to EURATOM and the European Coal and

Steel Community.

9. *Major Addresses . . . of General Charles de Gaulle, op. cit.,* pp. 92-93.

10. *Ibid.,* p. 120.

11. Newhouse, *op. cit.,* p. 145.

12. *Ibid.,* p. 221.

13. *Ibid.,* p. 225.

14. *Ibid.,* p. 227.

15. *Major Addresses . . . of General Charles de Gaulle, op. cit.,* pp.

16. Werth, *De Gaulle,* p. 331.

17. For a full discussion of the treaty and its ramifications, see Chapter 5.

18. For a full discussion of de Gaulle's reaction to the signing of the Nuclear Test Ban (Moscow) Treaty, see Chapter 5.

19. *Major Addresses . . . of General Charles de Gaulle, op. cit.,* p.

20. *Ibid.,* p. 22.

21. *Ibid.*

22. *Speeches and Press Conferences,* No. 224 (New York: French Embassy, June 17, 1965), pp. 3-4.

23. *Ibid.,* No. 228 (September 9, 1965), p. 7.

24. *Ibid.,* No. 239 (February 21, 1966), p. 4.

25. On April 8, 1965, the European Six signed a treaty to fuse the institutions of the EEC, EURATOM, and the European Coal and Steel Community (ECSC). It called for the fusion of the three governmental councils and the three commissions of these organizations into one governmental council and one commission.

26. *Speeches and Press Conferences,* No. 253 (October 28, 1966), pp. 1-2.

27. *Major Addresses . . . of General Charles de Gaulle,* March 17, 1964-May 16, 1967 (New York: French Embassy), p. 180.

28. "La Politique Etrangère de la France," *Notes et Etudes Documentaires,* Nos. 3487 à 3489 (Paris: La Documentation Française, 10 mai, 1968), p. 180. Translated by the author.

29. Although de Gaulle did not specifically say so, this was a clear-cut reference to Britain's external independence from the United States.

30. *Speeches and Press Conferences,* No. 216, p. 6.

31. For full discussion of the events of the spring of 1968, see Chapter 6.

32. Newhouse, *op. cit.,* p. 324.

33. *Ibid.,* p. 326.

Chapter 4

1. "A Summit Meeting," *International Affairs* (Moscow: Soviet Society for the Popularization of Political and Scientific Knowledge,

March, 1958), p. 72.

2. F. Courtade, "The Paris-Bonn Axis and the Future of France," *International Affairs,* July, 1959, p. 18.

3. "Les Relations Franco-Soviétiques," *Notes et Etudes Documentaires,* No. 3302 (6 juin, 1966), p. 7. Translated by the author.

4. *Major Addresses . . . of General Charles de Gaulle,* May 19, 1958-January 31, 1964, p. 43.

5. *Communiqué on Premier Khrushchev's Visit to France, March 23-April 3, 1960* (New York: French Embassy, 1960), p. 2.

6. De Gaulle reminded Khrushchev at the initial meeting of the summit conference that the USSR was flying satellites in outer space over French territory and the territories of other nations as well, a subject that Khrushchev promptly dropped.

7. *Major Addresses . . . of General Charles de Gaulle, op. cit.,* p. 77.

8. *Ibid.,* p. 76.

Chapter 5

1. "Les Relations Franco-Soviétiques," *Notes et Etudes Documentaires,* No. 3302 (6 juin, 1966), p. 14. Translated by the author.

2. *Ibid.*

3. *Ibid.*

4. *Ibid.,* p. 15.

5. Alvin Z. Rubinstein, ed., *The Foreign Policy of the Soviet Union,* 2nd ed. (New York: Random House, 1968), p. 294.

6. "Les Relations Franco-Soviétiques," *Notes et Etudes Documentaires,* No. 3302; p. 15. Translated by the author.

7. *Ibid.*

8. "Note du Gouvernement Soviétique au Gouvernement Français en Date du 5 février, 1963," *Articles et Documents,* No. 1357 (Paris: La Documentation Française, 26 février, 1963), p. 2. Translated by the author.

9. "Réponse du Gouvernement Français à la Note du Gouvernement Soviétique, 5 février, 1961," *Articles et Documents,* No. 0.1376 (13 avril, 1963), p. 1. Translated by the author.

10. "Texte de la Note du Gouvernement Soviétique au Gouvernement Français, 17 mai, 1963," *Articles et Documents,* No. 0.1393 (30 mai, 1963), p. 12. Translated by the author.

11. Werth, *De Gaulle,* p. 321.

12. *Major Addresses . . . of General Charles de Gaulle,* May 19, 1958-January 31, 1964, p. 237.

13. *Ibid.,* p. 238.

14. *Ibid.*

15. "Les Relations Franco-Soviétiques," *Notes et Etudes Documentaires*, No. 3302, p. 19. Translated by the author.

Chapter 6

1. "De Gaulle's Actions Lauded by Adzhubei," *New York Times*, April 8, 1964, p. 4.
2. "Les Relations Franco-Soviétiques," *Notes et Etudes Documentaires*, No. 3302, p. 22. Translated by the author.
3. "Pravda Asks Improved Paris Relations," *Washington Post*, October 28, 1964, p. A-10.
4. "Les Relations Franco-Soviétiques," *Notes et Etudes Documentaires*, No. 3302; p. 23. Translated by the author.
5. Michel Gorday, "Paris-Moscow Flirtation," *New Republic*, 152 (New York, May 15, 1965), 10.
6. *Ibid.*
7. *Ibid.*, p. 11.
8. "Gromyko Comes to Paris," *The Economist*, 215 (London, May 1, 1965), 509.
9. "Communiqué Franco-Soviétique, Publié de la Visite Effectuée en URSS, de 28 octobre au 2 novembre, 1965, par Couve de Murville," *Articles et Documents*, No. 0.1761 (16 novembre, 1965), p. 1. Translated by the author.
10. *Ibid.*
11. "Les Relations Franco-Soviétiques," *Notes et Etudes Documentaires*, No. 3302; p. 26. Translated by the author.
12. Hans E. Tutsch, "De Gaulle's Policy Toward the Communist East," *Swiss Review of World Affairs*, XV, 10 (January, 1966), 3.
13. Max Beloff, "President de Gaulle's Visit to the USSR," *The Listener*, 76 (London, July 14, 1966), 43.
14. *Ibid.*
15. W. W. Kulski, "The USSR-France-Germany," *The Russian Review*, 25 (October, 1966), 353.
16. *Ibid.*, pp. 353-354.
17. Beloff, *op. cit.*, p. 43.
18. Edmund Stevens, "Kosygin's Objective in Paris," *Washington Star*, December 1, 1966, p. A-6.
19. Henry Tanner, "Paris Sees a Loss in Its Prestige in Visit by Kosygin to London," *New York Times*, February 11, 1967, p. 8. cols. 7-8.

Chapter 7

1. "Les Relations Franco-Yougoslaves," *Notes et Etudes Documentaires*, No. 3773 (25 mars, 1971), p. 13. Translated by the author.

2. *Ibid.*, p. 14.
3. *Ibid.*
4. "La Politique Etrangère de la France," *Notes et Etudes Documentaires,* Nos. 3384 à 3387 (29 avril, 1967), p. 17. Translated by the author.
5. Yugoslavia, like the USSR, also espoused the policy of two German states in Europe.
6. "Les Relations Franco-Yougoslaves," p. 18. Translated by the author.
7. *Ibid.*
8. *Ibid.*
9. *Ibid.*
10. *Ibid.*
11. "Les Relations Franco-Roumaines," *Notes et Etudes Documentaires,* No. 3696 (9 juin, 1970), p. 9. Translated by the author.
12. *Manchester Guardian,* July 28, 1964, p.
13. "Les Relations Franco-Roumaines," p. 10. Translated by the author.
14. *Ibid.*
15. *Ibid.*
16. *Ibid.*
17. *Ibid.*, p. 13. Ceaucescu became president of Rumania in 1967. He had been party secretary since 1965, when Gheorghiu Dej died.
18. "Les Relations Franco-Polonaises (1945-1972)," *Notes et Etudes Documentaires,* No. 3922 (25 septembre, 1972), p. 16. Translated by the author.
19. *Ibid.*, p. 18.
20. *Ibid.*, p. 19.
21. *Ibid.*
22. *Ibid.*, pp. 19-20.
23. *Ibid.*, p. 20.
24. *Ibid.*
25. "La Politique Etrangère de la France," *Notes et Etudes Documentaires,* Nos. 3487 à 3489 (10 mai, 1968), p. 72 . Translated by the author.
26. Although the French and Polish positions on Vietnam were similar, they were not identical. The Polish position was identical to that of the USSR. For a fuller discussion of the French and Soviet positions on Vietnam, see p. 116.
27. "La Politique Etrangère de la France," *Notes et Etudes Documentaires,* Nos. 3487 à 3489, p. 122.
28. *Ibid.*
29. The USSR and Hungary voted against the resolution, while Algeria, India, and Pakistan abstained.
30. "La Politique Etrangère de la France," *Notes et Etudes Documen-*

taires, Nos. 3587 à 3589 (12 mai, 1969), p. 11. Translated by the author.

31. *Ibid.*, Nos. 3533 à 3535 (12 novembre, 1968), p. 92. Translated by the author.
32. *Ibid.*, p. 93.
33. *Ibid.*
34. *Ibid.*, Nos. 3384 à 3387 (29 avril, 1967), p. 155.
35. *Ibid.*

Chapter 8

1. It must also be remembered that three million Jews who lived in Poland prior to World War II lost their lives during the German occupation.
2. "La Politique Etrangère de la France," *Notes et Etudes Documentaires*, Nos. 3587 à 3589 (12 mai, 1969), p. 61. Translated by the author.

Bibliographical Note

Numerous writers throughout the world have written books in their native languages about the life of Charles de Gaulle. Most of these books are political biographies. The two books in this category I found most helpful are Alexander Werth, *De Gaulle* (Middlesex, England: Penguin Books Ltd., 1967), and Stanley Clark, *The Man Who Is France* (New York: Dodd, Mead, 1960). Both provide the reader with details of de Gaulle's early life so essential to the understanding of the ideas and contributions of this distinguished statesman in his later years.

Very important to the understanding of de Gaulle's ideas are his three most renowned books *Le Fil de l'Epée* (Paris: Librairie Berger-Levrault, 1932); *Vers l'Armée de Métier* (Paris: Librairie Berger-Levrault, 1934); *La France et son Armée* (Paris: Librairie Plon, 1938), and of course the *Complete War Memoirs of Charles de Gaulle* (New York: Simon and Schuster, 1959).

Since de Gaulle's treatment of the United States in his later years was in part conditioned by his relationship with Roosevelt during World War II, Milton Viorst's book *Hostile Allies: FDR and Charles de Gaulle* (New York: Macmillan, 1965) was most helpful in my understanding of de Gaulle's attitude toward the United States.

The two other books I found most informative, and which portray de Gaulle in very different lights, are John L. Hess, *The Case for de Gaulle* (New York: Morrow), and John Newhouse, *De Gaulle and the Anglo-Saxons* (New York: Viking Press, 1970). The latter is filled with much data often overlooked by political biographers of de Gaulle.

Among the documents I found most essential were *Major Addresses, Statements and Press Conferences of General Charles de Gaulle, May 19, 1958-January 31, 1964;* and *Major Addresses and Statements of General Charles de Gaulle Delivered Outside France, April 7, 1960-October 17, 1963.* These two documents are followed by *Major Addresses, Statements and Press Conferences of General Charles de Gaulle, March 17, 1964-May 16, 1967,* which combines the General's addresses and statements both inside and outside France. All three are published by the Press and Information Division of the French Embassy in New York.

La Documentation Française has published a series of documents under the title *Notes et Etudes Documentaires.* In this series, the researcher finds numerous pamphlets on French economics, politics, and foreign policy. I found these pamphlets most helpful in preparing the sections on de Gaulle's policy toward the USSR, Poland, Rumania, and Yugoslavia. Unfortunately La Documentation Française has not yet published pamphlets on Franco-Czechoslovak, Franco-Hungarian, and Franco-Bulgarian relations. La Documentation Française also publishes under the title *Notes et Etudes Documentaires* "La Politique Etrangère de la France," which is now published biyearly. This series was also of much assistance.

Among the basic documents I used was *Articles et Documents* published in Paris by La Documentation Française. In this series, the researcher finds numerous documents, including official letters exchanged between the French government and other governments throughout the world.

The Press and Information Division of the French Embassy in New York used to publish a file entitled *French Affairs*, and *Speeches and Press Conferences*. The former was very helpful in preparing the brief section in the book concerning the French economy at the time de Gaulle took office, but this file also contained information about political, social, and cultural, as well as economic, affairs. The latter was a series of documents that included not only the speeches and press conferences of the president of France but also those of the prime ministers, foreign ministers, and other important French governmental officials. However, neither series is published any longer under these titles. Since 1971, all of the series published by the Press and Information Division have been combined and appear by year and number, not by title.

La Revue Française de Sciences Politiques, Politiques Etrangères, and *Revue de Défense Nationale* are three French political science monthlies of the highest academic standard. They were most helpful in my preliminary research on this project.

Index